CRITICAL THINKING
AND INTELLIGENCE ANALYSIS
Occasional Paper Number Fourteen

DAVID T. MOORE

National Defense Intelligence College
Washington, DC
March 2007

CONTENTS

Figures and Tables

PREFACE

The world in which intelligence analysts work has changed dramatically over the 67 years since the beginning of the Second World War. Adversaries have shifted from large armies arrayed on battlefields to individuals lurking in the shadows or in plain sight. Further, plagues and pandemics, as well as floods and famines, pose threats not only to national stability but even to human existence. To paraphrase a Chinese curse, we certainly live in interesting times.

Our times demand fresh, critical reasoning on the part of those tasked to assess and warn about threats *as well as those tasked to act on those threats*. Education in the bases and practices of intelligence foraging and sensemaking – often called intelligence collection and analysis – is a means by which this can be accomplished. Indeed, the Intelligence Reform and Terrorism Prevention Act of 2004 legislates improved education for intelligence analysis. But, that education is not specifically defined. This volume provides a framework for one area of the act's educational requirement: improving how analysts think – and by extension, how policymakers act. It asserts that people who are skilled critical thinkers are better able to cope with interesting times than those who are not.

The model for thinking developed here also provides specific tools for coping with accelerating disruptive technologies. Such technologies routinely appear in the hands of adversaries. They also offer intelligence professionals capabilities to counter adversaries in novel ways. The key is knowing which technologies are truly disruptive in advance, which pose threats, and which can be harnessed to mitigate threats. Critical thinking – as it is here defined and developed – provides part of the solution as it encourages careful consideration of the available evidence, close examination of presuppositions and assumptions, review of the alternate implications of decisions, and finally, discussion of alternative solutions and possibilities. In short, it equips intelligence professionals with an essential tool for their work.

FOREWORD

Mark M. Lowenthal
Former Assistant Director of Central Intelligence
for Analysis and Production
President, Intelligence & Security Academy, LLC

Some years ago, when I worked at the Congressional Research Service, my colleague next door had a sign in his office: "Thinking is hard work. That's why so few people do it." Indeed. As sentient beings we think all the time. Our waking, conscious hours are full of thoughts: what to wear; what to eat; how to respond to someone. These all take thought. One might venture to say that we think almost unconsciously through most of our day.

And then there is that *other* thinking: Thinking about the conundrums that we face, the alternatives and choices we have to make on larger issues, the dilemmas we wish to resolve. This *is* hard work. And if the work you do is largely intellectual in nature, then you are thinking that much more often about these more difficult problems. This is not to suggest that those who work with their hands or in crafts or industry do not think. Of course they do. But these people, in the end, have something physical to show for their thought and its execution. Intellectuals only have their thoughts to show, presumably expressed for others in some way.

Intelligence officers are engaged in an intellectual pursuit. They are trying to solve puzzles, resolve uncertainties, discover the nature and meaning of things that others would keep secret. They must have an entire intellectual apparatus to help them identify the problem, assess the parts they know and the parts they do not, come up with an explanation of what is going on and then express it in a way that others – including an audience not steeped in their own techniques – can understand.

As one would expect, the Intelligence Community has spent a fair amount of time thinking about how it does analysis. But most of this has been spent on techniques, presentation and outcomes; much less has been spent on what happens intellectually while you are thinking. That, indeed, is what critical thinking is about: the ability to step out of one's thoughts, if you will, to examine them and the process that brought them about even while you are thinking them. It does not require some higher level of cosmic consciousness or a split personality. It does require training and thought! So now we are thinking about our thinking while we are thinking – a mental triple play, if you will. This is no mean feat and it is a very crucial skill for intelligence analysts.

John McLaughlin, a former Deputy Director of Central Intelligence, has observed that one of the major perceptions that separates intelligence officers from the policy makers is that policy makers tend to be optimists, believing they can get things done, while intelligence officers tend to be skeptics, knowing that little is known with certainty. Like everyone else, however, intelligence analysts can be adamant about their conclusions, understanding the path they took to reach them, and well-satisfied that they have done the right work and come to the right end. That is where critical thinking comes in. The ability to examine how you came to your conclusion is an important adjunct to your other intellectual work. You may be certain or you may not – which is also acceptable. But you owe it to yourself and to your readers to have examined how you got there.

This is not as easy as it sounds for intelligence analysts for the simple reason that they are usually very pressed for time. There are not a lot of lulls in the analyst's work week, which makes it very difficult to be introspective. This means that critical thinking ought to be something that is ingrained in analysts as part of their training, so that it becomes reflexive. But to do that, one must first understand critical thinking – what it is, how to do it, how to teach or learn it. That is the outstanding value of this monograph by David Moore.

The Intelligence Community is filled with people happily working away under a cloak of anonymity, satisfied in making their contribution to part of a larger activity about which very few beyond their immediate circle of co-workers will know. David Moore has long been one of these contributors. In addition to his duties as an intelligence officer at the National Security Agency, David Moore has devoted many fruitful hours to the intellectual underpinnings of intelligence, especially to what makes analysts and what makes better analysts. His work on analytic core competencies, written with his colleague Lisa Krizan, is a fascinating dissection of the intellectual attributes that make up an intelligence analyst. It was also a very influential work, becoming a prime motivator in the creation of the Analytic Resources Catalog created under Director of Central Intelligence George Tenet and now much touted by Director of National Intelligence John Negroponte.

This new monograph on critical thinking will serve a similar purpose. Much has been written in the last five years about intelligence and about the errors that it can make. Some of this has been diagnostic; much of it has been blithely condemnatory. Prescriptions about connecting dots better (an absurd metaphor), about the need to share information better and alarms about groupthink do not get us closer to improvements in the art, craft and profession of intelligence. New ways of thinking about our profession, new ways of doing our work and new ways of assessing it will be useful. Critical thinking needs to be at the top of this list of desiderata.

I would like to believe that we are on the verge of a renaissance in intelligence studies, and more specifically in the intellectual basis of intelligence analysis. There are many straws in the wind: discussions about a national intelligence university and a lessons learned center, more schools offering serious courses about intelligence and books like this. Critical thinking is and should be critical for all analysts and they will profit from this book.

COMMENTARY:

Jeffrey R. Cooper
SAIC Technical Fellow
Science Applications International Corporation

David Moore has written an elegant and largely persuasive argument for the Intelligence Community to move forthrightly and adopt critical thinking in order to improve the quality both of its analytic processes and its intelligence judgments. Since I have recently written about the need for the Community to identify and cure deep-seated and systemic "analytic pathologies," I am obviously sympathetic to the general case for incorporating more rigorous analytic processes—among which "critical thinking" is one attractive approach.[1] Along with Moore, I also believe strongly that the traits often associated with critical thinking need to become fundamental characteristics of every analyst and to be practiced consistently in their work habits. Moore discusses these aspects at some length and highlights their value to making sounder judgments.

In doing so, he makes a compelling case that critical thinking can help analysts reshape their methods in ways that help to avoid damaging errors and enhance judgment. He and I agree with Rieber and Thomason that we should validate the potential improvement before widespread deployment.[2] The need for validation raises some related points concerning the criteria for evaluation and measurement. As Philip Tetlock has noted, on the one hand, one can do evaluation by assessing whether a process (assumed to be good) has been followed; one the other hand, one can also assess

---

1 Jeffrey R. Cooper, *"Curing Analytic Pathologies: Pathways to Improved Intelligence Analysis"* (Washington, DC: Central Intelligence Agency, Center for the Study of Intelligence, 2005). Cited hereafter as Cooper, *Pathologies*.

2 Steven Rieber and Neil Thomason, "Toward Improving Intelligence Analysis: Creation of a National Institute for Analytic Methods," *Studies in Intelligence* 49, no. 4 (Winter 2006), 71.

quality by looking at the products themselves.[3] However, following a good process does not guarantee good products, nor does a good judgment necessarily validate the quality of the analysis or the analyst. Both approaches have flaws as methods of validation.

I urge the leadership of the Intelligence Community to place far more emphasis on structured analytic methods. In my view, the transformation of the intelligence enterprise demands a more curious, more agile, and more deeply thoughtful cadre of intelligence analysts—but it should also require the same traits among its intelligence organizations and the intelligence enterprise as a whole. Moore notes that "Investment in critical thinking as part of the analysis process minimizes the likelihood of specific failures" (page 81). However, from my perspective, critical thinking (and other structured methods) are more important for changing the organization's overall approach to analysis, rather than in improving specific judgments or preventing particular failures.

I believe such methods are crucial in preventing systemic analytic pathologies from developing, exactly because the Community lacks many of the desirable self-corrective mechanisms found in science. Second, while Moore focuses on the role of critical thinking in improving an individual analyst's ability to make good judgments, my view emphasizes the importance of more rigorous processes for the organization as a whole if it is to improve its capacity to meet user needs. Indeed, given my emphasis on the systemic nature of the pathologies that afflict intelligence analysis, structured analytic methods become a first line of defense in preventing networks of errors—they are like "ripstops" that keep problems from propagating into wider "error-inducing systems," in Perrow's terms. The quality of "mindfulness" and a more self-reflective process are essential if the intelligence organizations are to acquire some of the desirable characteristics of high-reliability organizations. While critical thinking can clearly assist individual analysts, and these "memes" can be spread through viral dissemination, I would place far more emphasis on fomenting social and organizational changes as remedies.

---

3 Philip E. Tetlock, *Expert Political Judgment: How Good Is It? How Can We Know?* (Princeton, NJ: Princeton University Press, 2005).

Finally, exactly because Moore focuses so tightly on the value of critical thinking to improve how individual analysts reason, he largely ignores the important role such habits should, and could, play in the "social construction" of intelligence analysis *and its communication to users of that intelligence.* The use of more structured techniques "to present more effective assessments" should go beyond simply convincing policymakers "to question their own assumptions on the issues" (page 80). By restructuring both the analytic process and the modalities of interactions with policy users, critical thinking techniques can draw policy users into "co-creating" important judgments and, by doing so, get them to adopt some of the important attributes of critical thinking. This internalization would be more powerful than hoping the exquisite brilliance of the improved analytic judgments might make them more palatable.

These minor quibbles aside, David Moore has highlighted for the Intelligence Community and its users some tangible methods for improving intelligence analysis and addressing systemic analytic pathologies.

COMMENTARY

Francis J. Hughes
Professor, National Defense Intelligence College

> The truly difficult problems of the information age are not technological; rather, they concern ourselves – what it is to think, to reason, and to engage in conversation [using] ... new analytic techniques, new conceptual tools with which to analyze and understand the workings of the human mind.
>
> —Keith Devlin, *Goodbye Descartes: The End of Logic and the Search for a New Cosmology of the Mind*, 1997

David Moore has undertaken a valuable initiative on behalf of the Intelligence Community by producing this monograph on critical thinking. In doing so, he has addressed the concerns of Keith Devlin and many other scholarly writers on the subject of human reasoning. By contextualizing the concept and practices of critical thinking within intelligence analysis, he has set forth a much-needed cognitive linkage between intelligence analysis and the human thought process, which, as he states, remains otherwise "poorly understood."

Mr. Moore has developed a methods-of-thinking course, outlined in the Appendix to this paper, which should guide the collection of evidence, the reasoning from evidence to argument, and the application of objective decision-making judgment. Critical thinking in intelligence depends primarily on a conscious application of suitable habits of thought, and the course certainly promises to advance the education of intelligence professionals.

COMMENTARY

Gregory F. Treverton
RAND Corporation
Former Assistant Director of Central Intelligence for
Analysis and Production
and Vice-Chairman, National Intelligence Council

David Moore has added his powerful voice to those calling for America's intelligence analysts to be more self-conscious about their methods and more venturesome in applying more formal methods. His starting point is critical thinking, but his strong case embraces a range of techniques from Paul and Elder's checklist, to analysis of competing hypotheses (ACH), to Factions analysis, which is really a way to be more systematic in aggregating subjective judgments, to techniques such as those developed by the Novel Intelligence from Massive Data (NIMD) project. These help analysts search for patterns and test hypotheses. Moore's discussion pays particular attention to critical thinking about *evidence* – that is perhaps natural given that the National Security Agency is his home agency, but it is also a welcome emphasis.

My own explorations of the analytic agencies over the last few years confirm my own experience managing the National Intelligence Council (NIC): In general, U.S. intelligence analysis has been neither very self-conscious about its methods, nor made much use of machines and formal analytic tools. That is Moore's point of departure, and it is a case made graphically by Rob Johnston, on whose work Moore draws. The state of affairs Moore and others describe is changing, and his work should contribute to accelerating that change, in a variety of experiments and pilot projects.

Moore's paper raises at least two intriguing questions at its edges. He rightly takes issue with Malcolm Gladwell's book about the power of unconscious thought or "deliberation without attention."

That said, clever defense lawyers often discredit ballistic experts by asking them to be explicit about how they reached their conclusions. Likewise, chess masters can be reduced to middle-weights by having to explain the logic of their moves. In both cases, the decisions result from patterns as much sensed as seen, the result of thousands of previous cases. I sometimes worried at the NIC that the more we required analysts to be explicit about their methods, the more we risked turning them into middle-weights.

Finding ways to incorporate not just expertise, but also hunch and sense into intelligence analysis is a challenge that lies ahead. The Defense Advanced Research Projects Agency's ill-fated experiment a few years ago seeking to establish a terrorism futures market was testimony to how hard the challenge will be. When the idea became public, every politician – right, left and center – quickly denounced it as borderline immoral. Over the ensuing days, however, a wide range of analysis commented on what a good idea it might have been when information is in short supply and there is a premium on sensing patterns before they become facts.

The second issue is consumers of intelligence, who figure only at the margins of Moore's discussion. We can only hope he is right that better analysis will find, and perhaps help create, a better audience. But the unboundedness of the terrorist threat we now face means that intelligence and policy no longer share a "story" comparable to that about state threats, like the Soviet Union. In principle, that would suggest that policy should accord more time and attention to intelligence, but that is not likely to happen in Washington's whirligig.

Thus, intelligence will need to be as creative in finding new ways to work and communicate with policy officials as it is in improving its analytic techniques. In the process, it will need to rethink what it regards as its *product*. I came to think at the NIC that our product was not really National Intelligence Estimates but, rather, National Intelligence *Officers* – people, not paper, and people in a position to come to know their policy counterparts and to make their expertise available informally, in meetings or at lunch.

ACKNOWLEDGMENTS

The first notes for this paper were begun a year prior to the 11 September 2001 terrorist attacks in New York and Virginia as part of research conducted with a peer, Lisa Krizan, on a set of core competencies – knowledge, skills, abilities, and an associated set of personal characteristics – for successful intelligence analysis. At the time, the notion of critical thinking was at best vaguely understood by members of the Intelligence Community, and the National Security Agency (NSA) was no exception. Six years later critical thinking is a recognized key skill by which intelligence readiness is defined at NSA. Similar growth in its importance is recognized elsewhere in the Community. This recognition is due in part to the work of Dr. Linda Elder, Dr. Gerald Nosich and Dr. Richard Paul, all of the Foundation for Critical Thinking. They have created a practical model for critical thinking that is both effective and easy to teach.

That the Paul and Elder model is known within the Intelligence Community is due in no small part to Professor Francis J. Hughes of the National Defense Intelligence College (NDIC). It was he who introduced the author to the model and encouraged attendance at Paul and Elder's annual conference on critical thinking. He kindly also provided a commentary on the paper. Dax Norman, of the NSA Associate Directorate for Education and Training, a number of NSA colleagues, and approximately 250 participants in the NSA critical thinking and structured analysis course helped make that course a reality and additionally provided valuable insights into the nuances of critical thinking. Comments from LT Robert D. Folker, USAF, also provided insight into the teaching of critical thinking. LT Folker developed a similar course while a student at the NDIC that unfortunately did not remain in the curriculum.

As the paper progressed, a number of colleagues and peers provided feedback, comments, and challenges to the arguments presented. They include, in alphabetical order, Solveig Brownfeld, NDIC; James Bruce, SAIC; Jan Goldman, NDIC; Mary Rose Grossman, the John F. Kennedy Presidential Library and Museum; Alexandra Hamlet; Noel Hendrickson, James Madison University;

Robert Heibel, Mercyhurst College; Richards J. Heuer, Jr., Central Intelligence Agency (retired); Norval J. Hilmer, Defense Intelligence Agency; LTCOL James Holden-Rhodes, USMC (retired); Morgan D. Jones, Central Intelligence Agency (retired); Hugo Keesing, Defense Intelligence Agency (retired); Mark Marshall, NDIC; Stephen Marrin, University of Virginia; Montgomery McFate, Institute for Defense Analysis; William Reynolds, Least Squares Software; the staff of the Central Intelligence Agency's Sherman Kent Center; and the staff of the John F. Kennedy Presidential Library and Museum. Several other colleagues at the National Security Agency – who wish to remain anonymous – also offered valuable insight and suggestions.

Three colleagues, Mark Lowenthal, president of the Intelligence & Security Academy, LLC; Jeffrey Cooper, Science Applications International Corporation; and Gregory Treverton, Rand Corporation, also deserve mention. Mark kindly agreed to write the foreword and offered valuable suggestions. His quip about really good analysts set up much of the arguments presented herein. Both Jeff and Greg provided critical comments and suggestions late in the game. They also kindly agreed to write commentaries on the paper.

Russell Swenson, Director of NDIC's Center for Strategic Intelligence Research and NDIC Press editor, did what a really good editor is supposed to do: His input and recommendations ensured that the arguments that follow were focused and strong. The Center's William Spracher also provided valuable technical editing services. Colleague Lisa Krizan provided a final review of the text that proved extremely valuable. This paper would not have been published if not for their dedicated assistance to the author.

Acknowledgment is due to four other people. Peter and Mary Moore encouraged their son to be inquisitive and to always look beyond the obvious for answers. Anthropologist John McDaniel first introduced the author – then a student at Washington and Lee University – to an analogy for intelligence sensemaking: science-based field archaeology. Finally, Elizabeth Moore provided tremendous encouragement. She also graciously tolerated the many nights and weekends spent writing, listening to, and commenting on, ideas as they occurred, sharpening the resulting arguments. It is to these people that this work is dedicated.

While the author was privileged to receive assistance of others, this remains his work and any errors are his. The author may be reached via electronic mail at dtmoore@nsa.gov.

CRITICAL THINKING
AND INTELLIGENCE ANALYSIS

DAVID T. MOORE

Examples included in this paper were selected to illustrate points raised by the author. No interest by the National Security Agency, the Department of Defense, or any other agency of the U.S. Government should be inferred from their inclusion.

ABSTRACT

Analysts and analysts alone create intelligence. Although technological marvels assist analysts by cataloguing and presenting data, information and evidence in new ways, they do not do analysis. To be most effective, analysts need an overarching, reflective framework to add structured reasoning to sound, intuitive thinking. "Critical thinking" provides such a framework and goes further, positively influencing the entire intelligence analysis process. Analysts who adopt critical thinking stand to improve their analyses. This paper defines critical thinking in the context of intelligence analysis, explains how it influences the entire intelligence process, explores how it toughens the art of intelligence analysis, suggests how it may be taught, and deduces how analysts can be persuaded to adopt this habit.

DEFINITIONS

Thinking – or reasoning – involves objectively connecting present beliefs with evidence in order to believe something else.

Critical Thinking is a deliberate meta-cognitive *(thinking about thinking)* and cognitive *(thinking)* act whereby a person reflects on the quality of the reasoning process simultaneously while reasoning to a conclusion. The thinker has two equally important goals: coming to a solution and improving the way she or he reasons.

Intelligence is a specialized form of knowledge, an activity, and an organization. As knowledge, intelligence informs leaders, uniquely aiding their judgment and decision-making. As an activity, it is the means by which data and information are collected, their relevance to an issue established, interpreted to determine likely outcomes, and disseminated to individuals and organizations who can make use of it, otherwise known as "consumers of intelligence." An intelligence organization directs and manages these activities to create such knowledge as effectively as possible.

CRITICAL THINKING
AND INTELLIGENCE ANALYSIS

INTRODUCTION: HOW DO PEOPLE REASON?

The best analytical tool remains a really good analyst.

—Mark Lowenthal, Former Assistant Director of
Central Intelligence for Analysis and Production

To create intelligence requires transformations resulting from an intellectual endeavor that sorts the "significant from [the] insignificant, assessing them severally and jointly, and arriving at a conclusion by the exercise of judgment: part induction, part deduction," and part abduction.[4] That endeavor is known as *thinking*, or "that operation in which present facts suggest other facts (or truths)."[5] Thinking – or as it is sometimes known, reasoning – creates an "objective connection" between our present beliefs and "the ground, warrant, [or] evidence, for believing something else."[6]

These three reasoning processes trace the development of analytic beliefs along different paths. Whereas inductive reasoning reveals "that something is probably true," deductive reasoning demonstrates "that something is necessarily true."[7] However, both are limited:

---

4 William Millward, "Life in and out of Hut 3," in F. H. Hinsley and Alan Stripp, *Codebreakers: The Inside Story of Bletchley Park* (Oxford, UK: Oxford University Press, 1993), 17. The author adds "abduction" for reasons that will shortly become evident.

5 John Dewey, *How We Think: A Restatement of the Relation of Reflective Thinking to the Educative Process* (New York, NY: D.C. Heath and Company, 1910), 12. Cited hereafter as Dewey, *How We Think.*

6 Dewey, *How We Think,* 12.

7 David A. Schum, "Species of Abductive Reasoning in Fact Investigation in Law," *Cardozo Law Review* 22, nos. 5–6, July 2001, 1645, emphasis added. Cited

inductive reasoning leads to multiple, equally likely solutions and deductive reasoning is subject to deception. Therefore, a third aid to judgment, abductive reasoning, showing "that something is plausibly true," can offset the limitations of the others.[8] While analysts who employ all three guides to sound judgment stand to be the most persuasive, fallacious reasoning or mischaracterization of rules, cases, or results in any of the three can affect reasoning using the others.

Inductive reasoning, moving from the specific to the general, suggests many possible outcomes, or the range of what adversaries may do in the future. However, inductive reasoning lacks a means to distinguish among each outcome – all are possible. An analyst has no way of knowing whether a solution is correct.

Deductive reasoning on the other hand, moving from the general to the specific, addresses questions about adversarial behavior and intentions. Deductive reasoning becomes essential for warning. Based on past perceptions, certain facts indicate specific outcomes. If, for example, troops are deployed to the border, communications are increased, and leadership is in defensive bunkers, then war is imminent. However, if leadership remains in the public eye then these preparations indicate that an exercise is imminent.

Abductive reasoning reveals plausible outcomes to the intelligence analyst. When an adversary's actions defy accurate interpretation through existing paradigms, abductive reasoning generates novel means of explanation. In the case of intelligence warning, an abductive process presents policy–making intelligence consumers with an "assessment of probabilities." Although abduction provides no guarantee that the analyst has chosen the correct hypothesis, the probative force of the accompanying argument indicates that the most likely hypothesis is known and that elusive, actionable intelligence is on tap.

---

hereafter as Schum, "Species." American mathematician, logician, semiotician, and philosopher Charles Sanders Peirce (1839–1914) developed the concept of abductive reasoning. See Joseph Brent, *Charles Sanders Peirce: A Life* (Bloomington, IN: Indiana University Press, 1998).

8 Schum, "Species," 1645.

Figure 1 models analysts' thinking about HUMINT received during the summer of 1962 regarding reports of foreigners in Cuba. An initial (fallacious) conclusion derived from inductive reasoning apparently was reapplied through deductive reasoning as explained in the case study incorporated in this paper.[9] Something else was needed – but not considered – to challenge the initial conclusion that "All HUMINT from Cuba was false."

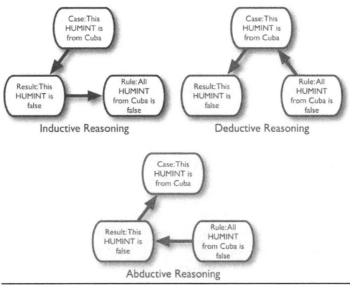

Figure 1: A Comparison of Inductive, Deductive, and Abductive Reasoning

Sources: Adapted from Thomas A. Sebeok, "One, Two, Three Spells UBER-TY," in Umberto Eco and Thomas A. Sebeok, *The Sign of Three: Dupin, Holmes, Pierce* (Bloomington, IN: Indiana University Press, 1988), 8; and James H. Hansen, "Soviet Deception in the Cuban Missile Crisis," *Studies in Intelligence*, 46, no. 1 (2002), 56.

If analysts can model an adversary's intentions based on observable actions, adversaries also can deduce how those analysts will have

9 While there is no evidence it was applied in the Cuban case, abductive reasoning is included in the figure for purposes of illustration.

moved toward these conclusions. Under these circumstances, the adversary then can engage in deceptive practices that can lead an intelligence service to misinterpret that adversary's intentions.[10] For example, the Indian government deceived the U.S. Intelligence Community before the former's 1998 nuclear test. Through a 1995 demarche from the U.S. government, the Indian government knew what indicators the U.S. sought and was able to obscure them until after the test. Then, the Indian government boasted of its success.[11]

Abduction forces a close consideration of the evidence at hand. Given competing estimates – such as "war is imminent" or "an exercise will occur" – the body of facts and inferences must be examined to determine "whether there are facts which falsify one of the estimates."[12] Only then can an assessment of accuracy be determined. Even then, the selected estimate remains only the "most likely."[13]

Despite their individual limitations, induction, deduction, and abduction taken together offer a means of thoroughly examining evidence in order to arrive at accurate intelligence conclusions. However, as becomes obvious from studying figure 1, in order to be successful, intelligence analysis requires something more: an overarching framework is needed to ensure reasoning relies on valid assertions, is not fallacious, and is self-consciously objective. Critical thinking provides that framework by ensuring that each form of reasoning is appropriately used. Critical thinking extends to the entire intelligence analysis process. The claim here is that analysts who

---

10   Isaac Ben-Israel explores the duality of estimation in considerable detail. See "Philosophy and Methodology of Intelligence: The Logic of the Estimate Process, *Intelligence and National Security* 4, no. 4 (October 1989), 660–718. Cited hereafter as Ben-Israel, "Logic of the Estimate Process."

11   Paul J. Raasa, "The Denial and Deception Challenge to Intelligence," in Roy Godson and James J. Wirtz, *Strategic Denial and Deception* (New Brunswick, NJ: Transaction Publishers, 2002), 178, 223–224.

12   Ben-Israel, "Logic of the Estimate Process," 668.

13   Cynthia M. Grabo, *Anticipating Surprise: Analysis for Strategic Warning* (Washington, DC: National Defense Intelligence College, 2002), 13.

become better critical thinkers will improve their analyses, helping to lessen the likelihood of intelligence failures. In the example above, critically thinking analysts would have questioned the generalizing of their initial conclusion by asking, "Was all the HUMINT from Cuba *really* false?" To avoid the tautological problem of equating quality analysis with the concept of "critical thinking" requires a careful assessment of cognition in the intelligence environment. The underlying question is "How can the intelligence analysts to whom Lowenthal's epigraph refers be 'really good'?"

WHAT IS CRITICAL THINKING?

Defining Critical Thinking

Defining critical thinking is a first step to understanding how it contributes to intelligence analysis. Richard Paul and Linda Elder, of the Foundation for Critical Thinking, consider it to be

> that mode of thinking – about any subject, content, or problem – in which the [solitary] thinker improves the quality of his or her thinking by skillfully taking charge of the structures inherent in thinking and imposing intellectual standards upon them.[14]

In other words, critical thinking is both a deliberate meta-cognitive *(thinking about thinking)* and cognitive *(thinking)* act whereby a person reflects on the *quality* of the reasoning process simultaneously while reasoning to a conclusion. The thinker has two equally important goals: improving the way she or he reasons and coming to a correct solution.[15]

To accomplish these goals, the reasoner requires assisting structures. Paul and Elder define eight elements of reasoning, shown in figure 2. These elements lead thinkers to ask focused questions about the topic being considered and the thinking process itself. Paul and Elder assert that whenever people reason, they do so for a purpose. This reasoning exists within a point of view and is shaped by both conscious and unconscious assumptions. Reasoning involves the creation of inferences based on conceptual frameworks about reality. These inferences are generated as people consider evidence necessary to answer questions or solve problems. Further, reasoning leads to decision points with implications – things that might happen

---

14   Richard Paul and Linda Elder, *The Miniature Guide to Critical Thinking Concepts and Tools*, 4th Edition (Dillon Beach, CA: The Foundation for Critical Thinking, 2004), 1. Cited hereafter as Paul and Elder, *Concepts and Tools.*

15   Exactly what is the "correct solution" is issue and context dependent. What is important here is that the process of reasoning is enhanced.

– and consequences – things that do happen once the decision has been made. Finally, Paul and Elder insist that "learning to analyze thinking requires practice in identifying the structures in use."[16]

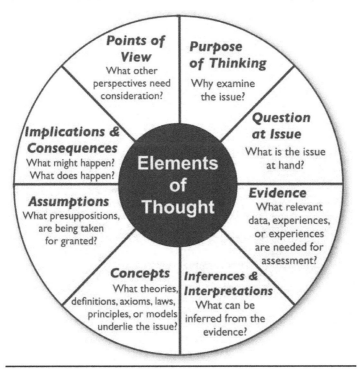

Figure 2: Elements of Thought

Source: Derived from Richard Paul and Linda Elder, *The Miniature Guide to Critical Thinking Concepts and Tools,* 4th Edition (Dillon Beach, CA: The Foundation for Critical Thinking, 2004), 2.

---

16 Linda Elder and Richard Paul, *The Foundations of Analytic Thinking: How to Take Thinking Apart and What to Look for When You Do* (Dillon Beach, CA: The Foundation for Critical Thinking, 2003), 5. Cited hereafter as Elder and Paul, *Analytic Thinking.* Paul and Elder, *Concepts and Tools,* 2.

Standards for Critical Thinking

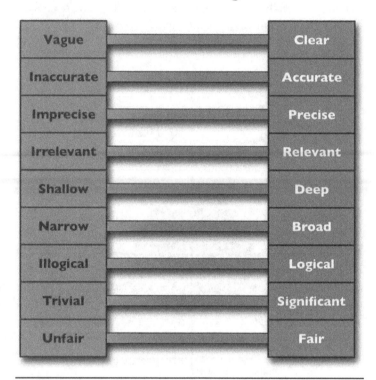

Figure 3: A Continuum of Intellectual Standards

Source: Derived from Paul and Elder, *Concepts and Tools*, 9.

Paul and Elder also establish a set of intellectual standards that offer criteria for assessing the level and quality of thinking. These form a continuum as shown in figure 3.[17] Active – or Socratic – questioning in a social setting becomes the means of critically exploring a topic or discipline as well as assessing the thinking on that topic. Questions assessing the issue delve into purpose, assumptions, inferences, as well as points of view on a topic.[18] Paul and Elder's

17   Elder and Paul, *Analytic Thinking*, 1–17.

18   Paul and Elder, *Concepts and Tools*, 2–9.

approach ensures that a topic or issue is thoroughly, logically, and objectively developed. Their continuum provides qualitative metrics to inform the thinker and others who may evaluate the object of the thinking along with the process employed. Each standard is related to but independent of the others. The object of consideration might be vaguely or clearly presented. But it also might be inaccurate. An example of this would be "the world is flat." This clear statement of reality is false.

The reasoning or its object might be clearly and accurately presented but remain imprecise, the level of detail required depending on the issue itself. Precision becomes important in assessing the location of an adversary or a threat as in "terrorists placed the improvised explosive device (IED) near the highway."

It is possible to create clear, accurate, and precise answers that are irrelevant. If one is considering the IED along the highway but the issue is how best to fly the troops in question from one location to another then the answer is irrelevant. Similarly, topics and their accompanying reasoning need to consider both the complexities involved (depth) and other points of view (breadth).[19] Such reasoning becomes essential when systems must be assessed because in systems "chains of consequences extend over time and many areas: The effects of action are always multiple."[20] Intelligence often must assess such systems – terrorist networks are but one example. Additionally, as sociologist Emile Durkheim observes, the combinations of elements related to an issue "combine and thereby produce, by the fact of their combination, new phenomena."[21]

When the correct phenomena or questions – and related alternative explanations – are not fully considered, intelligence failures occur. For instance, the Senate Select Committee on Intelligence

19   Elder and Paul, *Analytic Thinking*, 7.

20   Robert Jervis, *System Effects: Complexity in Political and Social Life* (Princeton, NJ: Princeton University Press, 1997), 10. Cited hereafter as Jervis, System Effects.

21   Emile Durkheim, *The Rules of Sociological Method* (Glencoe, IL: Free Press, 1938), xlvii.

found such reasoning to be among the causes of the Intelligence Community's failure to assess accurately Iraq's alleged programs to develop weapons of mass destruction (WMD). The senators noted that "Intelligence Community managers…did not encourage analysts to challenge their assumptions, fully consider alternative arguments, accurately characterize the intelligence reporting, or counsel analysts who lost their objectivity."[22]

Logic and significance also come into play. If the evidence presented does not imply the conclusions then the results are illogical. Focusing on appropriate evidence maintains significance. For example, evidence that terrorists who place an IED also have Stinger surface-to-air missiles bears on how troops can move across hostile territory.

Fairness deals with the agendas – hidden and expressed – of the thinker, her collaborative peers, and her customers. Knowing who has a stake in an issue as well as the stakes themselves helps ensure that issues are fairly reasoned and presented. Such considerations also reflect the analyst's own biases or opinions. In considering this point, Paul and Elder offer the evaluative question, "Am I misrepresenting a view with which I disagree?"[23]

Finally, while getting to the right-hand side of the spectrum on each of these standards in figure 3 is highly desirable, the standard of thinking on an issue will vary based on the skills of the thinkers and the issues under scrutiny. Assessing the resulting shortfalls in thinking reveals gaps that can be corrected. The continuum therefore provides a detailed assessment by which thinking on issues can be improved.

---

22   Senate Select Committee On Intelligence, *Report on the U.S. Intelligence Community's Prewar Intelligence Assessments on Iraq,* United States Senate, 108th Congress, 7 July 2004, 23. Cited hereafter as SSCI, *Iraq.*

23   Elder and Paul, *Analytic Thinking,,* 7.

Skill-Based Definitions

Other approaches to defining critical thinking focus on the specific skills. For example, Diane Halpern considers that

> [critical] thinking is the use of those cognitive skills or strategies that increase the probability of a desirable outcome. It is... thinking that is purposeful, reasoned, and goal directed – the kind of thinking involved in solving problems, formulating inferences, calculating likelihoods, and making decisions, when the thinker is using skills that are thoughtful and effective to the particular context and type of thinking task.[24]

Additional advocates of skills-based critical thinking include Edward Glaser and Alec Fisher, and their sets of critical thinking skills include a number of elements common to those identified by Halpern. The overlapping competencies of critical thinkers as advanced by Paul and Elder and these three other proponents are summarized in table 1. The comparison reveals the completeness of the Paul and Elder model.

These competencies assist intelligence analysts who contribute to the solution of threats to national security by ensuring the formulation of sound inferences about adversarial capabilities and intentions. Resulting findings are disseminated in reports that are often referred to as "assessments." At their best, they offer choices to decision-making consumers, as well as a clear outline of the implications of those choices.[25]

---

24 Diane Halpern, *Thought and Knowledge: An Introduction to Critical Thinking*, 4th Edition (Mahwah, NJ: Lawrence Erlbaum Associates, Publishers, 2002), 37. Cited hereafter as Halpern, *Thought and Knowledge*.

25 The term "assessment" describes the result of an intelligence production process but is not universally used within the Intelligence Community. Assessments are created at the Central Intelligence Agency and at the Defense Intelligence Agency. Other names for the reports that analysts produce include "products" at the National Security Agency (NSA) and "estimates" at the National Intelligence Council (NIC). Regardless of how they are named, they record and disseminate the results of analysts' work.

Competencies of Critical Thinkers	Paul and Elder	Fisher	Glaser	Halpern
Recognize problems or questions and find effective means of solution	✓		✓	✓
Engage in meta-cognitive activities that identify assumptions, biases, and performance as solutions are developed	✓	✓	✓	✓
Interpret data, appraise evidence, and evaluate statements in order to recognize logical relationships between propositions	✓		✓	✓
Infer warranted conclusions and generalizations from evidence	✓	✓	✓	✓
Test generalizations and conclusions by seeking out contradictory evidence that enables them to judge the credibility of claims	✓	✓	✓	✓
Convey sound, well-reasoned arguments	✓	✓	✓	✓
Focus on the process of reasoning with the intention of improving the process	✓			

Table 1: A Comparison of Different Sets of Critical Thinker's Competencies

Sources: Compiled by author from Linda Elder and Richard Paul, *The Foundations of Analytic Thinking: How to Take Thinking Apart and What to Look for When You Do* (Dillon Beach, CA: The Foundation for Critical Thinking, 2003); Diane Halpern, *Thought and Knowledge: An Introduction to Critical Thinking*, 4th Edition (Mahwah, NJ: Lawrence Erlbaum Associates, Publishers, 2002), 37; Edward M. Glaser, *An Experiment in the Development of Critical Thinking* (New York, NY: AMS Press, 1941), 6; and Alec Fisher, *Critical Thinking: An Introduction* (Cambridge, UK: Cambridge University Press, 2001), 8.

A Disposition to Think Critically

It is not enough merely to know the skills needed for critical thinking. To be successful, analysts as critical thinkers also need "certain attitudes, dispositions, passions, [and] traits of mind."[26] Actively thinking critically hones the skills; practice yields proficiency. But in order to gain mastery, willingness to reason in this manner becomes essential. The importance of this disposition to critically think cannot be over-emphasized. According to Peter A. Facione, Noreen C. Facione, and Carol A. Giancarlo, "Empirical studies…at multiple sites indicate that for all practical purposes" both critical thinking skills and the disposition to critically think are essential.[27]

There are a number of characteristics associated with the disposition to think critically. The Faciones and Giancarlo identify "seven characterological attributes or habits of mind… truth-seeking, open-mindedness, analyticity, systematicity, critical thinking, self confidence, inquisitiveness, and maturity of judgment."[28] According to Richard Paul and Gerald Nosich, the characteristics of critical thinkers include

> thinking independently, exercising fair-mindedness, developing insight into egocentricity and sociocentricity, developing intellectual humility and suspending judgment, developing intellectual courage, developing intellectual good faith and integrity, developing intellectual perseverance,

26 Richard W. Paul and Gerald Nosich, *A Model for the National Assessment of Higher Order Thinking*, (Dillon Beach, CA: Foundation for Critical Thinking, n.d.), 20. Cited hereafter as Paul and Nosich, National Assessment.

27 Peter A. Facione, Noreen C. Facione, and Carol A. Giancarlo, "The Disposition Toward Critical Thinking: Its Character, Measurement, and Relationship to Critical Thinking Skill," *Informal Logic* 20, no. 1 (2000): 61–84. Reprinted by Insight Assessment, URL: <http://www.insightassessment.com/pdf_files/J_Infrml_Ppr%20_2000%20–%20Disp%20&%20Skls.PDF>, last accessed 31 March 2006. Cited hereafter as Facione, "Disposition."

28 Peter A. Facione, Noreen C. Facione, Carol A. F. Giancarlo, *Professional Judgment and the Disposition Toward Critical Thinking* (Milbrae, CA: California Academic Press, 2002), URL: < http://www.calpress.com/pdf_files/Prof_jmn.pdf>, last accessed 31 March 2006.

developing confidence in reason, exploring thoughts underlying feelings and feelings underlying thoughts, developing intellectual curiosity.[29]

Both sets closely match the characteristics of successful intelligence analysts identified by Lisa Krizan and the author in their work on intelligence analysts' core competencies. Krizan and the author observe that successful intelligence analysts are insatiably curious. Fascinated by puzzles, their high levels of self-motivation lead them to observe and read voraciously, and to take fair-minded and varied perspectives. This helps them to make the creative connections necessary for solving the hardest intelligence problems. Finally, the emotional tensions created by problems, and the cathartic release at their solution, powerfully motivate analysts.[30]

In addition, emotions play a significant part in the process of critical thinking. As adult learning expert Stephen Brookfield observes, "[emotive] aspects – feelings, emotional responses, intuitions, sensing – are central to critical thinking."[31] He argues that the consideration of alternatives "to one's current ways of thinking" characterizes the approach.[32] Indeed, the consideration of these alternatives requires creativity, which he considers a non–rational form of thought.[33] Creative reasoning generates hypotheses; it has contributed significantly to the development of intellectual, scientific, and technological knowledge.

---

29 Paul and Nosich, *National Assessment*.

30 David Moore and Lisa Krizan, "Intelligence Analysis: Does NSA Have What it Takes," reprint NSA Center for Cryptologic History, *Cryptologic Quarterly* 20, nos. 1/2 (Summer/Fall 2001), 8–11. Cited hereafter as Moore and Krizan, "NSA,"

31 Stephen D. Brookfield, *Developing Critical Thinkers: Challenging Adults to Explore Alternative Ways of Thinking and Acting* (San Francisco, CA: Jossey–Bass Publishers, 1987), 12. Cited hereafter as Brookfield, Developing Critical Thinkers.

32 Brookfield, *Developing Critical Thinkers*, 12.

33 Brookfield, *Developing Critical Thinkers*, 12.

The Role of Questions

Greg Treverton observes that in intelligence the right questions rarely get asked.[34] Yet, critical thinking offers a means by which at least *appropriate* questions may be raised. The combination of critical thinking skills and the disposition to think critically focuses and directs inductive, deductive, and abductive reasoning to solve problems. This is an interrogative paradigm. Critical thinking involves questioning that forces broader consideration of issues and problems as well as the various means of resolving or answering them. Such questioning happens at both the individual and collective levels as shown in figure 4.

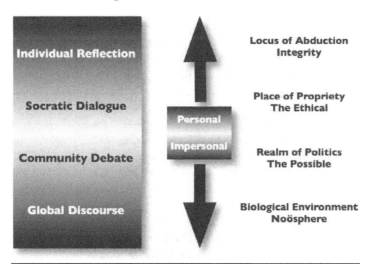

Figure 4: Levels of Questioning: Critical Thinking in a Social Setting

Source: Created by the author with contributions by Russell G. Swenson.

Questioning is either personal or impersonal and ranges from the musings of the individual critical thinker to that of a global discourse. As an individual ponders problems and issues, she abduces the most likely explanations. Moving up a level, questioning becomes a

34 Greg Treverton, conversation with the author, 18 April 2006.

hierarchical dialogue within dyads or larger assemblies. A critically thinking questioner ferrets out answers from others within the group. The process generates new questions that are answered in turn – and in turn, raise further questions. At the level of a community debate, critical thinkers explore what is possible politically and within the community's purview. Ideally, the relationship between thinkers is peer-to-peer. Finally, questions addressed within the context of a global discourse take into account the entire biological landscape (noösphere).[35]

Such questioning produces new and creative thinking, analogous to switching from Newtonian to quantum physics. In this analogy, an atomistic approach to analysis gives way to the associative impulse of synthesis as structured thoughts facilitate a leap to new questions, ideas, and possibilities. This overarching framework of structured reasoning frames questions to help analysts decide the best means or best combination of means that are suited to solving specific intelligence problems. The questions serve to alert an analyst to the notion that she might be deceived, or that she needs to employ some other means of reasoning to determine which of several alternative outcomes is most likely. These questions provide a formal means by which an analyst confronts her biases about likely outcomes. Therefore, in the context of intelligence analysis, critical thinking becomes one of the most – if not *the* most – important skills of the analyst. Facing symmetric and asymmetric threats, analysts have a potent and powerful tool to facilitate their asking the right questions in the process of improving their understanding of the problem at hand as well as their own reasoning about that problem.

Pseudo-Critical Thinking

It is important to understand what critical thinking is *not*. Critical thinking, as has been noted, focuses on both the process and the results of reasoning. However, the term is also used in reference to reasoning that is not reflective. The application of formal logic is sometimes (incorrectly) equated to critical thinking. So too are

35 Wikipedia defines the noösphere as the domain of human thought. Wikipedia, entry under "noösphere," accessed 27 February 2006.

problem solving and structured methods of analysis. Developers of school curricula and other exponents of "sound thinking" often lay claim to the mantel of critical thinking but are really leveraging their coverage of logic or problem solving to capitalize on an uncritical understanding of what critical thinking is. Problem solving, for example, focuses on answers and not on the process by which an answer is obtained. Additionally, logic or problem solving, being goal oriented, offer little means by which a person can improve the process of her thinking. The following problem is a typical example of pseudo–critical thinking:

> Two cyclists race along a straight course. The faster of the pair maintains an average speed of 30 mph. The slower cyclist averages 25 miles per hour. When the race ends, the judges announce that the faster cyclist crossed the finish line one hour before the slower racer. How many miles long was the racing course?[36]

This example (and others like it) focuses on the answer, provides no guidance on the process, and ignores any improvement in reasoning skills. Solvers either figure it out through trial and error or by following a rule-based strategy learned by rote. Therefore it fails to be critical thinking.

Unless the process, and the means, to improve a person's reasoning are emphasized, then at best such examples teach structured problem solving. At worst, they deal merely in criticism; they fail to assist people to learn to reason better. Central to critical thinking are the twin foci on the way in which a person is reasoning and the goal of improving that process. One could easily infer that misconceptions about critical thinking could be associated with what is taught as critical thinking in American educational institutions.[37]

---

36 Michael A. DiSpezio, *Classic Critical Thinking Puzzles* (New York, NY: Main Street, 2005), 85. The answer, by the way, is 150 miles (page 227).

37 Michael R. LeGault reaches this same conclusion in *Think: Why Crucial Decisions Can't Be Made in the Blink of an Eye* (New York, NY: Threshold Editions, 2006), 17. Cited hereafter as LeGault, *Think*.

WHAT CAN BE LEARNED FROM THE PAST? THINKING CRITICALLY ABOUT CUBA

Examining past intelligence successes and failures in light of new developments provides a means to reassess what happened and how outcomes could have been different. The case of the Soviet missiles in Cuba in the summer and fall of 1962 provides a means of examining how critical thinking and structured methodologies could have made a difference.

Deploying the Missiles

During the summer of 1962, CIA analysts received a spate of potentially alarming reports about Russians being seen in Cuba. The reports, however, were only part of a stream of similar, "farfetched tales of African troops with rings in their noses, lurking Mongolians, and even Chinese troops" on the island.[38] Most or all of these reports were discounted by analysts who were inured to spurious reports of Soviet equipment secreted away in caves.[39]

James Hansen – who worked in both the Central Intelligence Agency (CIA) and Defense Intelligence Agency (DIA) – posits that the U.S. Intelligence and Policy Communities were the victims of a concerted Soviet campaign of denial and deception that masked the deployment of Soviet forces and missiles into Cuba.[40] The deception campaign even included "accurate information about the deployment [leaked] so as to mask it."[41] As Raymond Garthoff relates, "there were literally thousands of reports of missiles in Cuba in the period *before* any missiles were actually brought there."[42]

---

38 James H. Hansen, "Soviet Deception in the Cuban Missile Crisis," *Studies in Intelligence* 46, no. 1 (2002), 56. Cited hereafter as Hansen, "Soviet Deception."

39 Hansen, "Soviet Deception," 56.

40 Hansen, "Soviet Deception," 49–58.

41 Domingo Amuchastegui, "Cuban Intelligence and the October Crisis," in James G. Blight and David A. Welch, Eds., *Intelligence and the Cuban Missile Crisis* (London, UK: Frank Cass, 1998), 101.

42 Raymond L. Garthoff, "US Intelligence in the Cuban Missile Crisis," in

In fact, the Soviets were able to deploy more than the offensive nuclear missiles that became the centerpiece of the subsequent crisis with the United States. While U.S. analysts and policymakers knew of the conventional weapons, they were blind to the presence of SS-4 Medium Range Ballistic Missiles (MRBM) and SS-5 Intermediate Range Ballistic Missiles prior to the U-2 overflights of 14 October. Additionally, it seems they never discovered the presence of approximately 100 tactical nuclear weapons deployed on the island.[43] There is debate whether U.S. Intelligence also *underestimated* the number of Soviet troops deployed to Cuba. Garthoff reports that one CIA unit concluded there were between 45,000 and 50,000 Soviet troops in Cuba (the actual number was about 42,000) but the official estimate was between 4,500 and 5,000 prior to the crisis.[44]

The Soviets employed an elaborate campaign of denial and deception that took advantage of American points of view about the likelihood of Soviet weapons being located in Cuba. As Robert Jervis makes clear,

> the U.S. did not expect the Russians to put missiles into Cuba or Japan to attack Pearl Harbor because American officials knew that the U.S. would thwart these measures if they were taken. These judgments were correct, but because other countries saw the world and the U.S. less accurately, the American predictions were inaccurate.[45]

It could have been worse. As Gil Merom writes, the Soviets might

---

James G. Blight and David A. Welch, Eds., *Intelligence and the Cuban Missile Crisis* (London, UK: Frank Cass, 1998), 22. Emphasis in original. Cited hereafter as Garthoff, "US Intelligence."

43   Garthoff, "US Intelligence," 29.

44   Garthoff, "US Intelligence," 28, 58. U.S. Intelligence never did reach a correct conclusion. The closest they got was an estimate of 22,000 troops in early 1963 (Garthoff, "U.S. Intelligence," 28).

45   Robert Jervis, *System Effects: Complexity in Political and Social Life* (Princeton, NJ: Princeton University Press, 1997), 45. Jervis draws on the work of Klaus Knorr. See Klaus Knorr, "Failures in National Intelligence Estimates: The Case of the Cuban Missiles," *World Politics* 16 (April 1964): 455–67.

have *completed* the bases and "threatened major U.S. cities with extinction."[46] The threat is brought home by figure 5.

What caused U.S. analysts to get it wrong? Apparently the U.S. analysts concluded that because some of the HUMINT evidence was ludicrous, all of it was. This inductive conclusion then led them to discount further evidence. For example, having concluded that all the previously considered Cuban HUMINT was false, each new piece, *since it came from Cuba,* also had to be false. Thus, a false inductive conclusion led subsequently to false deductive conclusions.[47] It does not appear that abductive reasoning strategies were ever employed.

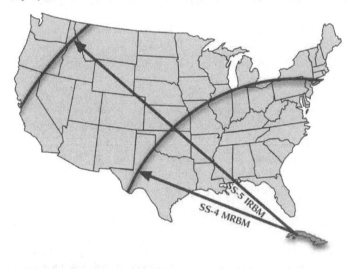

Figure 5: Respective Ranges of Soviet SS-4 MRBM and SS-5 IRBM Missiles

Source: Derived from Hansen, "Soviet Deception," 49.

46 Gil Merom, "The 1962 Cuban Intelligence Estimate: A Methodological Perspective," *Intelligence and National Security* 14, no. 3 (Autumn 1999), 49. Cited hereafter as Merom, "Estimate."

47 Inductive and deductive reasoning were illustrated in figure 1.

It should be noted that the U.S. Intelligence Community was not blind to the possibility that the Soviets might conduct a military buildup in Cuba. In fact, there were two theories being debated: One, that the Soviets would emplace *defensive* weapons, and the other that they would emplace *offensive* weapons. Senior analysts in the Intelligence Community held the former theory while John McCone, then Director of Central Intelligence, favored the latter.

Part of McCone's reasoning had to do with the cost and utility of the installation of SA-2 air defense missiles. McCone apparently reasoned that the purpose of installing such expensive missiles had to be greater than merely denying the United States overflight capabilities (the SA-2 could shoot down – as Francis Gary Powers discovered – a U-2).[48] This led McCone to come "up with an answer that no one wanted to hear: the SA-2s were on the island to deny the United States the capability to see the construction of offensive missile installations."[49]

Unfortunately, McCone was unable to dissuade the majority from their point of view. This may have stemmed, as James Blight and David Welch write, from the realization that while McCone's inference seemed reasonable when viewed in hindsight, in foresight it was faulty because it failed to sufficiently cover the alternatives.[50] Blight and Welch observe that

> the Soviets had also deployed SA-2 missiles to Egypt, Syria, and Indonesia, and in none of those cases had they also deployed strategic nuclear weapons. Indeed, the US intelligence community [sic] expected that the Soviet Union

---

48   Thomas R. Johnson and David A. Hatch, *NSA and the Cuban Missile Crisis* (Fort Meade, MD: National Security Agency Center for Cryptologic History, 1998), URL: <http://www.nsa.gov/publications/publi00033.cfm>, last accessed 18 April 2006. Cited hereafter as Johnson and Hatch, *NSA*.

49   Johnson and Hatch, *NSA*.

50   James G. Blight and David A. Welch, Eds., *Intelligence and the Cuban Missile Crisis* (London, UK: Frank Cass, 1998), 5. Cited hereafter as Blight and Welch, Intelligence and the Cuban Missile Crisis.

would deploy SA-2 missiles to Cuba, precisely because it had done so elsewhere.[51]

Even though history proved McCone to be correct (for the wrong reasons), the defensive weapons theory predominated.[52]

The Soviets took advantage of the American beliefs and faulty reasoning. Capitalizing on the idea that it is easier to lead a target astray than to try to change his mind, they successfully placed the nuclear missiles in Cuba.[53] Heuer observes that

> [deceptions] that follow this principle seldom fail, for the odds are then strongly in favor of the deceiver. The human capacity to rationalize contradictory evidence is easily sufficient to outweigh the pernicious effects of security leaks and uncontrolled channels of information that planners of deception...might compromise their efforts.[54]

Assessing the Implications

Exactly what happened in the Cuban case and does it apply to contemporary issues? Roberta Wohlstetter notes in retrospect, "We would like to know not only how we felt, but what we did and what we might have done, and in particular what we knew or what we could have known."[55] Wohlstetter's musings lead to two key questions for analysts: How could this successful deception campaign have been

51 Blight and Welch, *Intelligence and the Cuban Missile Crisis*, 5.

52 Merom, "Estimate," 58.

53 Richards J. Heuer, Jr., "Strategic Deception and Counterdeception: A Cognitive Process Approach," *International Studies Quarterly* 25, no. 2 (June 1981), 200. Cited hereafter as Heuer, "Strategic Deception." It is interesting to speculate whether the Soviets had a feedback channel that informed them of the predominant theory.

54 Heuer, "Strategic Deception," 200.

55 Roberta Wohlstetter, "Cuba and Pearl Harbor: Hindsight and Foresight," *Foreign Affairs* 46, no. 3 (July 1965), 691. Cited hereafter as Wohlstetter, "Cuba."

thwarted? What can be learned to advise analysts about current adversarial denial and deception?

Simply looking at additional evidence is sometimes promoted as a means of detecting denial and deception by adversaries. In the Cuban case, however, analysts had already processed a superabundance of evidence. Wohlstetter suggests that such riches can be "embarrassing."[56] This is because even as "signals" point

> to the action or to an adversary's intention to undertake it, "noise" or a background of irrelevant or inconsistent signals, [and] signs pointing in the wrong directions…tend always to obscure the signs pointing the right way.[57]

HUMINT assets overwhelmed analysts' abilities to distinguish signals from noise. Heuer and Hansen agree that once "locked in," analysts resist changing their minds. More evidence alone fails to change an analyst's mind because "[new] information is assimilated to existing images."[58] Yet, analysts stand to benefit from changing their opinion in the face of disconfirming evidence.

The limitations of hindsight analysis notwithstanding, if analysts had employed critical reasoning in 1962 they could have detected the Soviet *maskirovka* in Cuba. For example, by applying Paul and Elder's model of critical thinking, analysts would have had a means to question their assumptions and points of view, and subsequently might have questioned the purpose of the apparent "noise" they were discounting as well as their assumptions about the prevalent point of view that the Soviets would not place missiles on the island because we would react. Gil Merom suggests that some appropriate questions would have included: "How aware were the analysts of their own assumptions? Were these assumptions sensible and was it sensible to adhere to them?"[59] Other considerations that critical

---

56 Wohlstetter, "Cuba," 691.

57 Wohlstetter, "Cuba," 691.

58 Heuer, *Psychology*, 10–11.

59 Merom, "Estimate," 57.

thinking about the crisis might have raised are included in table 2. Applying Paul and Elder's model reveals other considerations that conceivably would have led to an earlier detection of the likelihood of the deployed weapons being *offensive*.

Would this approach have allowed detection of what the Soviets were doing in Cuba before mid-October 1962? One could argue counterfactually that it might have enhanced analysis of collection from other sources.[60] SIGINT assets capable of collecting Russian communications were in place near the island.[61] Imagery assets might have been tasked differently prior to 14 October. Sources less subject to generating noise would have introduced inconsistencies to an analysis of competing hypotheses that was solely HUMINT-based.

Between Dogmatism and Refutation

A systematic approach to directed collection also would have moved analysts toward a disconfirmatory analytic approach. By contrast, a confirmatory approach, often characterized as confirmation bias, leads analysts to accept what they set out to confirm.[62] A disconfirmatory approach aims to refute alternative

---

60 Counterfactual reasoning explores differing outcomes arising from alternative causes. Counterfactuals are commonly used in whenever alternate hypotheses are explored. They are essential for both post-mortem reviews and futures scenario exercises. See Philip E. Tetlock, and Aaron Belkin, *Counterfactual Thought Experiments in World Politics: Logical, Methodological, and Psychological Perspectives* (Princeton, NJ: Princeton University Press, 1996), 1–38. In the same volume, Richard Ned Lebow and Janice Gross Stein conduct a counterfactual review of the Cuban missile crisis. See Richard Ned Lebow, and Janice Gross Stein, "Back to the Past: Counterfactuals and the Cuban Missile Crisis," in Philip E. Tetlock, and Aaron Belkin, *Counterfactual Thought Experiments in World Politics: Logical, Methodological, and Psychological Perspectives* (Princeton, NJ: Princeton University Press, 1996), 119–148.

61 Johnson and Hatch, *NSA*. According to the authors, SIGINT played a key role in determining the operational status of the SA-2 air defense missiles. However, SIGINT failed to detect the delivery and installation of the nuclear missiles.

62 Wikipedia defines confirmation bias as "a type of cognitive bias toward confirmation of the hypothesis under study." (Wikipedia, entry under "confirmation bias").

Purpose	· Determine what is going on in Cuba as a part of the U.S. "war" against Castro and the Cuban communists.
Key Questions	· If this really is a Soviet military buildup, what kinds of weapons are being deployed: offensive weapons or defensive weapons? · Why is an expensive missile system like the SA–2 being installed in Cuba? · What is the SA–2 really protecting? · Does a crisis exist?
Evidentiary Considerations	· If defensive weapons are being deployed, what evidence should be observed? · If offensive weapons are being deployed, what evidence should be observed? · What is not being seen?
Inferences	· What is inferred from the observed and collected evidence?
Assumptions	· What is being assumed about the evidence? · What is being assumed about the sources of the evidence? · What is being assumed about why the Soviets would deploy weapons to Cuba?
Concepts	· How does human perception affect the analysis? · How reliable are the sources of evidence? (Could also be an assumption.)
Implications and Consequences	· If conclusions are incorrect about the Soviet build up, what might occur next? · If conclusions are correct about the Soviet build up, what can be expected? · If conclusions are incorrect about offensive weapons being deployed, what happens next? · If conclusions are incorrect about defensive weapons being deployed, what happens next?
Points of View	· What other points of view about what is going on in Cuba exist?

Table 2: Applying Paul and Elder's Critical Thinking Model to the Situation in Cuba, August–September 1962.

Source: Developed by author.

hypotheses. Whatever was left at the end of the process would be the most likely explanation. Would this guarantee a correct "answer"? Ben-Israel concludes that although the answer has to be "no," the approach does allow for narrowing "the margin of error."[63] It does so by moving the analyst away from a "pole of dogmatic tenacity" toward a "pole of refutation" (summarized in figure 6).[64]

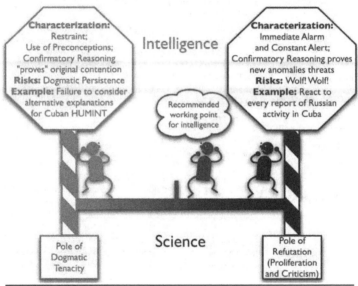

Figure 6: A Place for Analysis between Dogmatism and Criticism

Source: Derived from Ben-Israel, "Methodology of Intelligence," 679.

It should be noted that operating too closely to a pole of refutation can also create problems. For example, analysts might be unable to distinguish between real threats and false positives; they might react to each one regardless of its validity. In the Cuban case, this problem would have manifested itself in goading continual U.S. military reactions to every perceived Soviet and Cuban threat. Here again,

---

63 Ben-Israel, "Logic of the Estimate Process," 679

64 Ben-Israel, "Logic of the Estimate Process," 691.

critical thinking could moderate this Cassandrian approach.[65] The questioning of assumptions and points of view in critical thinking allows analysts to *discount* certain evidence. Based on his own Israeli intelligence analyst experiences, Ben-Israel asserts that anchoring oneself some distance from a pole of refutation, and not far from the center, is probably best.[66] In other words, enlightened skepticism probably works as a method for distinguishing between real and perceived threats. Critical thinking leads one to assess the processes one is using and the point on the continuum from which to work.

Lacking: Disconfirmation

Merom confirms that a disconfirmatory process did not occur on the Cuban missile problem: "Information that was inconsistent with the prevailing conservative theory was not considered as alarming and necessitating revision, but rather was 'rehabilitated' and rendered 'harmless' on the basis of *ad hoc* statements."[67] Instead, inductive reasoning generally led analysts to "prove" their theory and subsequently to adhere to it *"until it was proven wrong* by conclusive hard evidence" – the U–2 photos, to be exact (of which a detail is reproduced in figure 7).[68]

---

65 Cassandra was the daughter of Priam, King of Troy. She was blessed and cursed by the god Apollo to accurately predict the future yet never be believed. In intelligence, a Cassandrian approach is characterized as one that emphasizes dire outcomes and worst–case scenarios. Analysts who produce such assessments are often discounted and rarely thanked when they are correct. For a real account of how such warnings are perceived (at least at the time they are made), see Charles E. Allen, "Intelligence: Cult, Craft, or Business?" in *Seminar on Intelligence, Command, and Control, Guest Presentations,* Spring 2000 (Cambridge, MA: Harvard University Program on Information Resources Policy, I–01–1, April 2000), URL: <http://www.pirp.harvard.edu/pubs.html>, last accessed 11 January 2006.

66 Ben-Israel, "Logic of the Estimate Process," 679.

67 Merom, "Estimate," 69.

68 Merom, "Estimate," 69. Italics in original.

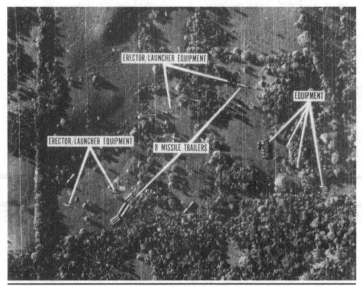

Figure 7: Detail of a U-2 Photograph of an SS-4 MRBM Launch Site, San Cristobal, Cuba, 14 October 1962. This evidence confirmed that Soviet missiles were being installed in Cuba.

Source: U.S. Department of Defense, photograph in the John Fitzgerald Kennedy Library, Boston, MA, PX 66–20:7 14 October 1962.

What tipped off the overhead surveillance were two HUMINT reports of "a Soviet truck convoy that appeared to be towing ballistic missiles toward the San Cristobal area."[69] That these reports were taken seriously is one of the curious serendipities that occur from time to time in intelligence analysis (and other research-based domains). What prompted the CIA and DIA analysts to take these reports seriously while earlier accounts had been dismissed remains a mystery. Garthoff asserts that it was new information taken in context with the observed "pattern of SA-2 surface-to-air missile sites in Western

---

69 Graham Allison and Philip Zelikow, *Essence of Decision: Explaining the Cuban Missile Crisis,* 2nd Edition (New York, NY: Longman, 1999), 220. Cited hereafter as Allison and Zelikow, *Essence of Decision.* Raymond Garthoff also notes this to be the case. See Garthoff, "US Intelligence," 23.

Cuba" that led to the tasking of the U-2 flight on 14 October (the track of which is shown in figure 8).[70]

Also contributing to the determination that the deployed missiles were SS-4 MRBMs was information transmitted to the British and American intelligence services by Oleg Penkovsky. While Penkovsky's espionage apparently did not warn the Americans that the Soviets were about to deploy offensive missiles in Cuba, he is credited with – among other things – providing technical information about the missiles.[71] Len Scott observes that Penkovsky provided the technical information that allowed the determination that the missiles were SS-4s instead of SS-3s, as well as information that allowed accurate assessment by the Americans of their readiness. Scott writes that this was important because

> the SS-3 had a range which US intelligence estimated at 630 nautical miles (nm), enabling coverage of seven Strategic Air Command (SAC) bomber/tanker bases; the 1020nm SS-4 could target 18 bomber/tanker bases (plus one ICBM complex), and some 58 cities with a population of over 100,000, including Washington, accounting for 92 million people.[72]

Shortly thereafter Penkovsky was detected, arrested, tried, and executed by the Soviets for his espionage.

---

70 Garthoff, "US Intelligence," 23.

71 Len Scott, "Espionage and the Cold War: Oleg Penkovsky and the Cuban Missile Crisis," *Intelligence and National Security* 14, no. 3 (Autumn 1999), 33. Cited hereafter as Scott, "Penkovsky."

72 Scott, "Penkovsky," 34. In making this assertion Scott draws on work previously published by Allison and Zelikow in *Essence of Decision* and by Mary S. McAuliffe, ed., *CIA Documents on the Cuban Missile Crisis, 1962* (Washington DC: Central Intelligence Agency, 1992).

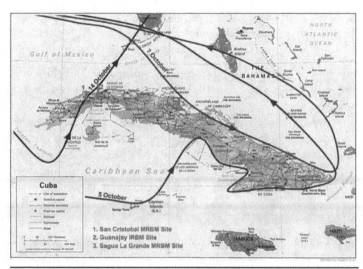

Figure 8: U–2 Tracks over Cuba, 4–14 October 1962.

Sources: Map, Central Intelligence Agency. Tracks derived from a map
in Mary S. McAuliffe, ed., *CIA Documents on the Cuban Missile Crisis, 1962*
(Washington DC: Central Intelligence Agency, 1992), 3. Hereafter McAuliffe. Missile locations derived from Arthur C. Lundahl, "Additional Information – Mission 3102," Memorandum for Director of Central Intelligence
and Director, Defense Intelligence Agency, 15 October 1962, in McAuliffe,
181–182; and Arthur C. Lundahl, "Additional Information – Mission 3107,"
Memorandum for Director of Central Intelligence and Director, Defense
Intelligence Agency, 19 October 1962, in McAuliffe, 209. Track and missile
locations are approximations. Lundahl was the Director, National Pho-
tographic Interpretation Center. The 19 October memo reports that a 5
September U–2 overflight did not detect the latter two missile sites. However, a review of the 5 September track (as presented in McAuliffe) shows the
aircraft only came near the Sagua La Grande site. It should also be noted
that the track of the U-2 – as flown on 14 October – deviated from the original planned route (which was farther to the west). The track as flown took
the aircraft closer to the San Cristobal site. What might have happened had
the original track been flown?

Despite their efforts at denial and deception, there was an evident
lack of concealment of the missiles by the Soviets prior to their
"discovery" on 14 October. General Anatoli Gribkov, a member
of the Soviet General Staff in Cuba at the time relates,

A missile–launching complex is not easily disguised...[Such] an installation...could be hidden from ground-level view. But from above, however, it could and did stick out like a sore thumb.[73]

Allison and Zelikow note that the Soviets only began to camouflage the sites *after* "the U.S. announced the discovery of the missiles and announced the blockade."[74] They conclude that the Soviet forces building the bases lacked personnel and resources to conceal them – a situation that apparently changed only after the missiles had been discovered.[75]

The Roles of Critical Thinking in the Cuban Crisis

Merom's critique of the Intelligence Community's estimate of Soviet intentions vis-à-vis Soviet weapons in Cuba reveals areas that would be well-served by critical thinking. First, when a critical thinking paradigm is in control, intelligence foraging and gathering are efficiently oriented. Questions are raised about the existing evidence – both anomalous and consistent – as well as where new disconfirming and confirming evidence might be discovered. Second, alternative – what in the context of Cuba, Merom calls *revolutionary* – theories are considered.[76] A structured process also speeds up the process of analytic sensemaking: estimates are crafted earlier.[77] Third, a methodological process opens analysis to "guiding principles of

---

73 Anatoli Gribkov, "The View from Moscow and Havana," in Anatoli Gribkov and William Y. Smith, *Operation ANADYR: U.S. and Soviet Generals Recount the Cuban Missile Crisis* (Chicago, IL: Edition Q, 1994), 39. Cited hereafter as Gribkov, "The View."

74 Allison and Zelikow, *Essence of Decision*, 208.

75 Allison and Zelikow, *Essence of Decision*, 214.

76 Merom, "Estimate," 71.

77 Structured processes provide a framework that reduces the flailing around as analysts seek to find a starting point for their analyses. Morgan Jones discusses this at some length. See Jones, *Thinker's Toolkit*, xi–xvi.

research," enriching both the process and the results.[78]

However, there are dangers to such a paradigm, especially as "science" commonly is understood. As Jeffrey Cooper notes, "a 'science of analysis' is a conceit, partly engendered by Sherman Kent's dominating view of intelligence as a counterpart of the scientific method."[79] Mark and Barbara Stefik argue that "the working methods of science and invention leaves [sic] out imagination. This makes it both boring and misleading."[80] Analysts must focus on both evidence and inferences; otherwise they can "get the details right at the cost of ignoring important inferential judgments that need to be conveyed in order to provide a true sense of the uncertainties of both evidence and judgment."[81] Here again, critical thinking, with its emphasis on creative questioning, moderates the process. Such questioning opens the way for imaginative thinking. "[Intuition], curiosity, and a thirst for discovery – all essential elements of good science" could have alerted analysts working in 1962 (or at any other time) to the possibility that they were being denied or deceived.[82]

An interesting intersection exists between critical thinking and analogy, or drawing comparisons to derive new patterns and explanations. This intersection lies at the heart of creativity.[83] According to Keith Holyoak and Paul Thagard, there are commonly four steps to analogical problem solving:

> Often a problem solver will select a source analog by retrieving information about it from memory (*selection*), map the source to the target and thereby generate inferences about the target

78 Merom, "Estimate," 57.

79 Cooper, Pathologies, 26..

80 Mark Stefik, and Barbara Stefik, *Breakthrough: Stories and Strategies of Radical Innovation* (Cambridge, MA: MIT Press, 2004), 110.

81 Cooper, *Pathologies*, 27.

82 Cooper, *Pathologies*, 31.

83 This statement illustrates just how pervasive and powerful the use of analogy is in human reasoning and discourse. Taken literally, creativity has no heart (nor any other organs) since it is a notion or a concept, not a living animal. Yet the analogy to a living being aids understanding.

(*mapping*), evaluate and adapt the inferences to take account of unique aspects of the target (*evaluation*), and finally learn something more general from the success or failure of the analogy (*learning*).[84]

Since analogy is such a powerful element in human reasoning, how can critical thinking outwit or control it? As developed in this paper, it does so by imposing a structure on the thinking. By examining inferences and implications as well as alternative points of view, critical thinking calls into question the appropriateness of the analogies in use. Recent work by Paul and Elder reveals how this works. They request, for example, that reasoners state and restate explanations, add examples, and then include an analogy.[85] While initial statements about a phenomenon *do not* imply understanding, restatement, examples, and analogies *do* and further, provide measures by which comprehension can be fixed and assessed; they make knowledge explicit – something that can be thought about.[86] When knowledge and reasoning are explicit, assumptions are revealed.

According to Richard Neustadt and Ernest May, it is known that analogy is a tool commonly invoked by policymakers.[87] Critically thinking analysts can add substantively to the policymakers' options by constructively challenging the tendency to rely upon analogy as a way of addressing situations. For example, Neustadt and May observe that in coping with the missile crisis in Cuba, President Kennedy and his advisers relied on – among other things – an analogy to Pearl Harbor to justify why a "surprise" bombing of the Soviet missile

---

84   Keith J. Holyoak and Paul Thagard, *Mental Leaps: Analogy in Creative Thought* (Cambridge, MA: The MIT Press, 1995), 15. Emphasis in original. Cited hereafter as Holyoak and Thagard, *Mental Leaps.*

85   Richard Paul and Linda Elder, "Instructions to Participants," 25th Annual Conference on Critical Thinking, Berkeley, California, 9 July 2005. The first three elements were developed previously; analogy was new in 2005.

86   Holyoak and Thagard, *Mental Leaps, 20–22.*

87   Richard E. Neustadt and Ernest R. May, *Thinking in Time: The Uses of History for Decision Makers* (New York, NY: The Free Press, 1986). Cited hereafter as Neustadt and May, *Thinking in Time.*

bases was *not* a satisfactory option.[88] Kennedy's advisers, acting as analysts of the situation, critically evaluated the appropriateness of the analogy, pointing out its weaknesses and strengths. Kennedy concluded that sneak attacks were not a tactic lying within the U.S. tradition.[89]

In the Cuban case, getting analysts to restate their conclusions, provide examples, and make analogies would have revealed the strengths and weaknesses of their arguments about what they observed from the HUMINT sources. It would have shown their comprehension of what they wanted to conclude, revealed their assumptions and, in so doing, opened an avenue for "alternative" assessments of the issue. It would have done so by causing the analysts to question how it was that they failed to notice or ignore things.[90] The stage would have been set for an earlier, less risky, defusing of the impending crisis.

Another analogy employed in the Cuban missile crisis was the comparison to the Soviet position vis-à-vis the presence of *American* MRBMs in Turkey. A critical review reveals that the Soviet Union had tolerated the presence of these missiles – which had a longer range than those placed in Cuba – since 1957.[91] If the U.S. demanded the removal of the Soviet missiles from Cuba, was not a similar withdrawal of the American missiles from Turkey appropriate? Ultimately, this analogy provided a face-saving solution for the Soviet Union in the negotiations that followed. As a "secret" part of the agreement, the American Jupiter MRBMs were removed from Turkey five months after the Soviet Union removed its missiles from Cuba.[92]

---

88 Neustadt and May, *Thinking in Time*, 6.

89 Neustadt and May, *Thinking in Time*, 7.

90 Margaret A. Boden, *The Creative Mind: Myths and Mechanisms* (New York, NY: Basic Books, 1990), 25.

91 Neustadt and May, *Thinking in Time*, 9.

92 Neustadt and May, *Thinking in Time*, 15.

Winners and Losers: The Crisis in Context

A Critical Assessment of the Leaders. In any confrontation there are winners and there are losers. Thinking critically about the confrontation over the Soviet missiles also involves determining who actually won as well as what the other outcomes might have been. Each of the three actors, Castro, Khrushchev, and Kennedy, had a number of interests at stake. In a number of circumstances each stood to gain at the expense of the others. What solutions were the most advantageous to each of the three actors? What were the motivating factors? A speculative – and admittedly simplified – critical comparison, again using Paul and Elder's model (summarized in table 3) illustrates how critical thinking also reveals much about who stood to gain and who stood to lose in the crisis.

Castro. Castro found his country under attack from the United States – both directly through economic sanctions and indirectly by Batista loyalists living in Florida.[93] The previous year the United States had launched an invasion attempt at the Bay of Pigs – which was repulsed. However the attempts by the United States to destabilize or overthrow the Cuban government did not end with their defeat. As Raymond Garthoff observes, "by the spring of 1962 the United States had embarked on a concerted campaign of overt and covert political, economic, psychological, and clandestine operations to weaken the Castro regime...including attempts to assassinate Castro."[94] In short, the United States was doing everything *except* conventional warfare to destroy Castro and his regime.

Castro's point of view was that the United States was a real enemy. He could reasonably assume that in light of its other activities and having attempted an invasion once, the United States would repeat its actions and this time *might* succeed (an implication). Another possible outcome that probably was considered was that war, conventional or nuclear, was likely. Castro must have possessed evidence of the military capabilities of the United States and probably inferred that

---

93 Raymond L. Garthoff, *Reflections on the Cuban Missile Crisis* (Washington, DC: The Brookings Institution, 1989), 7. Cited hereafter as Garthoff, *Reflections.*

94 Garthoff, *Reflections,* 9.

Element of Thinking	Considerations as seen from Castro's Point of View
Purpose	· Preserve Regime
Point of View	· United States threatens regime
Assumptions	· A second invasion will be attempted
Implications	· Invasion might succeed · War: conventional or nuclear
Evidence	· U.S. armed forces formidable
Inferences	· U.S. can overcome unaided Cuban forces.
Concepts	· Military strategy and doctrine, communist and capitalist theories
Key Questions	· How to deter United States from invading island

Table 3: A Comparative Assessment of Rival Motivations

Source: Developed by author.

Considerations	
as seen from Khrushchev's Point of View	as seen from Kennedy's Point of View
· Protect Cuba from United States · Force concessions from United States · Remove U.S. and NATO from Berlin · Spread Communism · Preserve Regime	· Get the missiles out of Cuba · Defend U.S. and allies against Communism · Preserve Regime
· United States a threat to Communism · Cuba threatened with invasion	· Communism threatens United States · Missiles are a threat
· Missiles in Cuba bargaining points · Missiles in Cuba protect Castro · Effort will be successful.	· Small Soviet Force · Strategy of removal is possible
· U.S. concessions · War: conventional or nuclear	· Successful removal · Escalation of measures · War: conventional or nuclear
· U.S. armed forces formidable	· Administration politically vulnerable over crisis · Khrushchev is a formidable adversary · Khrushchev is bluffing
· U.S. can overcome unaided Cuban forces. · Missiles provide necessary aid · United States will concede.	· Khrushchev will back down · Military option not required
· Military strategy and doctrine, communist and capitalist theories	· Military strategy and doctrine, communist and capitalist theories · Monroe Doctrine
· How to deter United States from invading Cuba · How to dominate the United States	· How to get the Soviets and their missiles off of Cuba

unaided, his own forces were no match for the U.S. forces. Underlying Castro's considerations were a number of ideas about military strategy and doctrine, as well as communist and capitalist theories. A corollary consideration commonly believed by many Americans (at the time and still today) might have been how Communism could have been spread across the Western Hemisphere, especially the United States. Castro's key question was, "How can I prevent the United States from invading again?"

Khrushchev. What motivated Khrushchev remains controversial. His motives certainly were more complex, as various explanatory hypotheses reflect. First, there is the argument that Khrushchev had an ally "in the faith" to protect. He too believed that the United States would invade Cuba a second time.[95] However, as Allison and Zelikow counsel, the troop buildup itself and *not* the nuclear missiles was what Khrushchev did to offset the perceived threat to Cuba from the United States.[96] The deployment of the nuclear missiles was related to some other issue.

Next, the situation posed an opportunity to force concessions from the United States – perhaps about Berlin, or the United States' own offensive missiles located in Europe and Turkey. Allison and Zelikow find sufficient evidence to lead them to believe that removing the U.S. and NATO troops from Berlin was a key factor motivating Khrushchev to deploy the missiles to Cuba.[97] Securing his borders from the American's Jupiter missiles may have been an additional motivating factor.

Additionally, there was Khrushchev's avowed purpose of spreading Communism across the globe. In this context the deployment of weapons lies within the context of "a great power rivalry... between the U.S. and the values and interests it represented...and

95 James J. Wirtz, "Organizing for Crisis Intelligence: Lessons form the Cuban Missile Crisis," in Blight and Welch, *Intelligence and the Cuban Missile Crisis,* 130. Cited hereafter as Wirtz, "Organizing."

96 Allison and Zelikow, *Essence of Decision,* 87.

97 Allison and Zelikow, *Essence of Decision,* 99–109.

the Soviet Union's communist agenda."[98] At a reception for foreign ambassadors in Moscow in 1956, Khrushchev threatened, "Whether you like it or not, history is on our side. We [the communists] will bury you!"[99] This remark (among others) also reveals an additional purpose: Khrushchev, like all dictators, had to appear stronger than his adversaries – his political survival depended on it.

Khrushchev's point of view was that the United States (and its allies) were a threat to Communism everywhere and needed to be contained. He was presented with a confluence of opportunities and responded with the military buildup in Cuba and the deployment of the missiles. He apparently assumed that if he could get nuclear missiles into Cuba he'd have bargaining points useful in such a containment strategy. Later, Khrushchev believed he could effect a change in the balance of power between the two nations.[100] Possible outcomes included the prospect of further U.S. concessions, protection of Cuba from invasion, and either conventional or nuclear war.

Khrushchev had direct evidence drawn from the Korean War and possibly other evidence from spies operating in the United States about the capability of the U.S. military. Given the nuclear missiles he actually deployed as well as his assignment (temporary) of operational control of those missiles to the Soviet Group of Forces commander, General Issa Pliyev, Khrushchev seems to have inferred the U.S. forces were formidable.[101] He also apparently concluded that the missiles – and the other forces – would be adequate to the task of successfully satisfying his purposes; the United States, faced with

---

98 Allison and Zelikow, *Essence of Decision*, 88.

99 Nikita Khrushchev, "Speech to Ambassadors at Reception, 17 November 1956," in James Beasley Simpson, compiler, *Simpson's Contemporary Quotations: The most Notable Quotes since 1950* (Boston, MA: Houghton Mifflin Company, 1988), online edition, URL: <http://www.bartleby.com/63/83/183.html>, last accessed 20 April 2006. Ironically, Khrushchev was wrong. History sided with his adversaries.

100 Cited in Garthoff, *Reflections*, 23.

100 Gribkov, "The View," 4. Control reverted back to Moscow in September.

operational missiles in Cuba, would concede.[102] The concepts on which Khrushchev relied probably were the same as those on which Castro relied: military strategy and doctrine as well as communist and capitalist theories. Again, Khrushchev's key question mirrored that of Castro: How to keep the Americans from invading Cuba. Additionally, there could have been a second question on how to dominate, or at least gain concessions from, the United States.

Kennedy. Finally, there was Kennedy. While Kennedy's exact purpose vis-à-vis Cuba *prior* to the discovery of the missiles also remains unclear, it is known that he did not plan to invade the island during the summer and fall of 1962.[103] However, 1962 was an election year and the Kennedy administration was vulnerable with respect to Cuba.[104] Kennedy could not afford to appear soft on Communism. Kennedy also had an interest in keeping the U.S. and NATO forces in Berlin.

All this changed once the missiles were discovered. Kennedy's deliberations revolved around removing the missiles as expeditiously as possible. He no doubt realized that if his administration bungled the crisis they might lose at the polls in November.[105] Therefore, it is reasonable to conclude that Kennedy's goals included retaining control of Congress – he too had a regime to preserve. Kennedy's point of view was clear: the deployed Soviet strategic nuclear missiles were a threat to the United States and must be removed. He assumed that such a strategy could be developed. He apparently also assumed that the Soviets had placed a *small* force on the island. Possible outcomes included successful removal of the missiles and their

---

102   Wirtz, "Organizing," 128. Wirtz argues that the Soviets were not only wrong about the U.S. reaction, they were *surprised!*

103   Wirtz, "Organizing," 130.

104   Fen Osler Hampson, "The Divided Decision-Maker: American Domestic Politics and the Cuban Crises," *International Security* 9, no 3 (Winter 1984/85), 136. Cited hereafter as Hampson, "Divided."

105   Hampson, "Divided," 143.

supporting forces, an escalation of measures to prompt that removal, and the possibility of conventional or nuclear war.[106]

Kennedy had evidence of his political vulnerability. He also had evidence – Khrushchev's own actions included – that the Soviet leader was a formidable adversary. But based on Penkovsky's evidence he inferred that Khrushchev might be persuaded to back down. As Scott concludes, "various writers contend that Penkovsky's intelligence…[guided] Kennedy's handling of the crisis from a position of strength."[107] This occurred in part because "the KGB's discovery of Penkovsky's espionage alerted Khrushchev to the fact that Kennedy now knew he was bluffing."[108] As has been noted, Kennedy lacked accurate evidence about what was really on the island. Nevertheless as has been noted, he inferred that military strikes were not – at least at that time – an option. Kennedy probably relied on the same concepts on which Castro and Khrushchev relied. In addition, the concepts embodied in the Monroe Doctrine were also probably a factor. Kennedy's key question was, "How to get the Soviets and their missiles out of Cuba?"

Foresight. Viewed with foresight, there were a number of possible outcomes to the crisis based on the inferrable goals that could be associated with any of the three leaders. A win for one of the leaders was not necessarily a loss for the others as table 4 shows. In some cases, achieving one's goal was a win for the leader, but a failure to achieve it was *not* necessarily a loss. "Winning" the crisis should have involved attaining all or most of one's goals. However, since not all goals were of equal importance, failing to achieve one could mean that one lost in the larger crisis. Similarly, achieving one's goals did not guarantee winning the larger crisis. This becomes evident as the actual winners and losers are considered.

---

106 Neustadt and May, *Thinking in Time*, 6-15. Given the presence of the Soviet tactical nuclear weapons on Cuba it is probable that *any* invasion that began with conventional forces would have escalated to nuclear scenarios.

107 Scott, "Penkovsky," 31.

108 Scott, "Penkovsky," 32.

And the Winner is? Who actually won the Missile Crisis? Critical assessments of the three leaders involved and the attainment of their goals reveals the answers. First, Castro certainly got what he wanted: The United States never again invaded Cuba.

What did Khrushchev get out of the resolution of the crisis? From the standpoint of his first goal, to protect Cuba from the United States, he was successful. The subsequent removal of the Jupiter

Goal	Outcome	Leader		
		Castro	Khrushchev	Kennedy
Prevent U.S. Inva-	Achieve	Win	Win	Neutral
sion of Cuba	Fail	Lose	Lose	Win
Get the Missiles	Achieve	Neutral	Lose	Win
out of Cuba	Fail	Win	Win	Lose
Spread Commu-	Achieve	Win	Win	Lose
nism	Fail	Neutral	Lose	Win
Get U.S. and Allies	Achieve	Neutral	Win	Lose
out of Berlin	Fail	Neutral	Lose	Win
Force Concessions	Achieve	Win	Win	Lose
from United States	Fail	Lose	Lose	Win
Force Concessions	Achieve	Neutral	Lose	Win
from Soviet Union	Fail	Neutral	Win	Lose
Force Concessions	Achieve	Lose	Neutral	Win
from Cuba	Fail	Win	Win	Neutral
Preserve Regime	Achieve	Win	Win	Win
	Fail	Lose	Lose	Lose

Table 4: Goals and Outcomes in the Cuban Missile Crisis

Source: Developed by author.

missiles in Turkey appeared to increase the security of his borders – an apparent concession from the United States.[109] However, Khrushchev failed to spread Communism further. And Berlin remained partially

---

109 The issue of the Jupiter missiles is complex. They were not included in the formal agreement but were offered up in a secret unilateral assurance from Kennedy (Garthoff, *Reflections*, 132).

in the hands of the West. If, as Allison and Zelikow postulate, this was the real motivation behind the nuclear deployment then Khrushchev's failure was highly significant. Additionally, his regime was embarrassed by the revelation in the United Nations of the presence of the missiles. Ultimately, he was removed from power two years later and placed under house arrest until his death in 1971. So, Khrushchev, while he won a number of his goals, wound up the overall loser.

Kennedy is the other winner in the crisis. He gets the Soviets missiles removed from Cuba while avoiding war. He is later able to retire an obsolete missile system (the Jupiters). He prevents the Soviet Union from seizing control of Berlin. Finally, his popularity increases and the Democrats retained power in the 1962 elections.

Ten Years Later, They Meet Again

It is worth noting that Soviet denial and deception in support of military deployments and operations in Cuba did not end in the early winter of 1962. In 1970 Henry Kissinger stormed into the office of H. R. Haldeman and demanded to see President Nixon. Aerial reconnaissance had brought news. "The Cubans are building soccer fields," Kissinger said. "Cubans play *baseball*. *Russians* play soccer."[110] The Soviets it seems had been discovered building a submarine base at Cienfuegos. Prior to a particular overflight, that fact had been denied to the United States. The soccer fields were for the recreation of Soviet troops.

---

110   H.R. Haldeman, with Joseph DiMona, *The Ends of Power* (New York, NY: Times Books, 1978), 85–86, in Patrick J. Haney, "Soccer Fields and Submarines in Cuba: The Politics of Problem Definition," *Naval War College Review* L, no 4, sequence 360 (Autumn 1997), URL: <http://www.nwc.navy. mil/press/Review/1997/autumn/art5–a97.htm>, last accessed 6 April 2006. Emphasis in original.

Judgment: Critical Thinking Would Have Made a Difference

As this case study makes clear, there are a number of junctures where critical thinking or structured analytic methods could have made a difference in analyzing the Soviet missile deployment to Cuba. While it is true that Sherman Kent argued for a scientific approach to analysis, it does not seem to have been widely practiced at the time.[111] As of 1962, most studies that we now have in hand on human reasoning in intelligence had not been completed. The champions of structured intelligence analysis methods had not yet developed their techniques.

Nevertheless, a study of the crisis is germane because the same kinds of errors *repeat themselves again and again.* The errors seen in the Cuban case – failure to question assumptions, to take seriously the evidence and the patterns they imply, to counterfactually examine analytic implication and consequences, in short to make reflective judgments – also were cited by the Senate in its critique of the 2002 Iraqi WMD estimate.[112] In both cases, deceptions confounded analysts, leading them to wrong conclusions.[113] In the Cuban case the analysts eventually figured it out. This did not occur in the

---

111 Sherman Kent, *Strategic Intelligence for American World Policy* (Princeton, PA: Princeton University Press, 1949), 151–208.

112 In the Cuban situation, the debate between McCone and analysts over the nature of the weapons the Soviets might emplace came close to overcoming these errors. Regarding the Iraqi WMD estimate, the debate between the CIA and the Department of Energy over the use of the aluminum tubes also came close. Unfortunately, the incipient debate focused on the results, not the process. In both cases, the side that was eventually proved right failed to make the now-accepted case.

113 Sherman Kent challenged this assertion in his defense of the original estimate and the process by which it was created. He believed that an earlier revelation of the Soviet actions would have led to an intractable situation. However, an earlier revelation – say in August – would have offered President Kennedy and his advisers more options, particularly more *diplomatic* options. Kent also failed to observe that denial and deception occurred – at least for the record. See Sherman Kent, "A Crucial Estimate Relived," Reprint, *Studies in Intelligence* 36, no. 5 (1992): 111–119.

most recent failure. Critical thinking skills went unused among both generations of analysts.

How Can Intelligence Analysts
Employ Critical Thinking?

The Poor Record

Critical thinking is what consumers of intelligence appear to expect when they task producers to examine issues. Corporate consumers require analysts creating intelligence to "[evaluate] a situation, problem, or argument and [choose] a path of investigation that leads to finding the best possible answers."[114] In the national security field, strategic intelligence pioneer Washington Platt notes that "[intelligence] is a meaningful statement derived from information which has been selected, evaluated, interpreted, and finally expressed so that its significance to a current national policy problem is clear."[115] Derived from strategic intelligence, "best answers" should clearly express what is significant to national policy problems. They may also support warfighters with essential operational and tactical intelligence. Critical thinking leads to the best answers for the specific context at hand.

Unfortunately, analysts' biases and mindsets repeatedly obscure best questions and answers. From well before the Japanese surprise attack on Pearl Harbor to the 2002 estimate on Iraqi weapons of mass destruction, a failure to think critically about potential crises contributed to repeated intelligence failures.[116] "Expert analysis"

---

114 Daniel Feldman, *Critical Thinking: Strategies for Decision Making* (Menlo Park, CA: Crisp Publications, Inc, 2002), 4.

115 Washington Platt, *Strategic Intelligence Production: Basic Principles* (New York, NY: Frederick A. Praeger, 1957), 8.

116 George S. Pettee, *The Future of American Secret Intelligence* (Washington, DC: Infantry Journal Press, 1946). Chapter 1 provides a summary of U.S. intelligence failures during the first half of the 20th Century. While hindsight is an imperfect mirror for reviewing the past, one conclusion to be drawn from a review of the evidence is that critical thinking could have minimized many of the ensuing crises.

was not enough.[117] Biases and mindsets too often converted subject-matter confidence into arrogance; false assumptions blinded analysts to their target's true intentions. For example, at least one CIA Iraq analyst acknowledged that the 1990 invasion of Kuwait,

> was an intelligence failure…We were guilty of a kind of mindset…The idea that a country [Iraq] would march up to the border, put 100,000 troops there, go in and do what they've done; I don't think anybody thought they'd do it.[118]

In 2002, Intelligence Community analysts failed to definitively assess whether the Iraqi government still possessed weapons of mass destruction. The Senate noted in its review of the failure that

> [rather] than thinking imaginatively, and considering seemingly unlikely and unpopular possibilities, the Intelligence Community instead found itself wedded to a set of assumptions about Iraq, focusing on intelligence reporting that appeared to confirm those assumptions.[119]

The mistakes of 2002 also occurred in 1990 – and for that matter in 1941. Analysts failed to question assumptions widely held at the time. Instead they chose the first answer that satisfied the situation, a phenomenon known as "satisficing."[120] Other means by which intelligence analysts and policymaking customers reasoned poorly are listed in table 5. According to Ephraim Kam, the problem is so great that the intelligence analysis process is "consistently biased, and…bias

---

117   Anthropologist Rob Johnston explores this paradox. See Dr. Rob Johnston, *Analytic Culture in the U.S. Intelligence Community: An Ethnographic Study* (Washington, DC: Center for the Study of Intelligence, 2005), 64–66. Cited hereafter as Johnston, *Analytic Culture.*

118 Anonymous CIA Analyst, 1990, in Don Oberdorfer, "Missed Signals in the Middle East," *Washington Post Magazine,* 17 March 1991, 40.

119 The Commission on the Intelligence Capabilities of the United States Regarding Weapons of Mass Destruction, *Report to the President of the United States,* March 31, 2005, URL: <http://www.wmd.gov/report/index.html>, last accessed 28 July 2005, 155. Cited hereafter as WMD Commission, *Report.*

120   Morgan D. Jones, conversation with the author, 15 December 2003.

is the cornerstone of intelligence failures."[121] Paul and Elder claim that much thinking is "biased, distorted, partial, uninformed, or down-right [sic] prejudiced."[122] There are repeated failures to think critically; but could critical thinking about these situations prevent the failures?

Means by Which Decisions are Made
Select first answer that appears "good enough."
Focus on narrow range of alternatives, ignoring need for dramatic change from existing position.
Opt for answer that elicits the greatest agreement and support.
Choose the answer that appears most likely to avoid some previous error or duplicate a previous success.
Rely on a set of principles that distinguish "good" alternatives from "bad" alternatives.

Table 5: How Analysts Decide

Source: Excerpted from Alexander George, *Presidential Decisionmaking in Foreign Policy: The Effective Use of Information and Advice* (Boulder, CO: Westview Press, 1980), Chapter 2.

Critical thinking helps mitigate the effects of mindsets and biases by invoking skillful examination of evidence both for and against an issue, as well as consideration of obvious and less obvious alternative explanations. In the 1990 example, thinking critically would have raised other possible explanations for why Hussein's troops were on the Kuwaiti border and what he intended for them to do.[123] That the Iraqi troops were trained by the former Soviet Union and followed its tactics might have been an indicator of future intentions. In the case of the weapons of mass destruction (WMD), analysts might have

---

121 Ephraim Kam, Surprise Attack: The Victim's Perspective (Cambridge, MA: Harvard University Press, 1990), 85.

122 Paul and Elder, *Concepts and Tools*, 1.

123 A consideration of who trained Hussein's troops – in this case, the Soviet Union – might have led to an examination of military doctrine. Thus, it quickly would have become clear that troops mobilized on a border were going to cross that border. Analysts would then have known that an invasion of Kuwait was imminent.

asked, as they realized they had no new evidence of the weapons, "How can we prove that the weapons of mass destruction definitely are not there?" or "What would we expect to see if Saddam Hussein had gotten rid of his weapons of mass destruction?"[124]

We must assume that analysts can be encouraged to think in this manner. Modern strategic intelligence pioneer Sherman Kent believed this to be the case when he wrote nearly 60 years ago that intelligence analysts "are supposed to have had more training in the techniques of guarding against their own intellectual frailties" than the larger populace.[125]

Assessing Evidence[126]

Understanding how evidence is assessed is a necessary first step in understanding how analysts can better reason with and about it. The incomplete and ambiguous information and data with which intelligence professionals work compounds their reasoning process.[127] Sources are unreliable and contradictory; adversarial denial and deception increase doubt. When information and data are questionable, derived evidence is even more uncertain, and inferences arising from that evidence may be highly suspect. One way that analysts can reduce this uncertainty is by building defensible inferences

---

124   These analyses are those of the author. The last question was jointly arrived at in a conversation between the author and Mark Lowenthal, 26 July 2005.

125   Sherman Kent, *Strategic Intelligence for American World Policy* (Princeton, NJ: Princeton University Press, 1949), 199.

126   This section is based (with additions) on materials developed by Francis J. Hughes and the author for a structured analytic methods course taught at the National Defense Intelligence College. For a deeper examination of evidence assessment see Francis J. Hughes and David A. Schum, *Credibility Assessment: A First Step in Intelligence Analysis,* unpublished tutorial, National Defense Intelligence College, April 2003.

127   Information, data, and evidence are different kinds of knowledge. Pieces of information comprise data, which in turn comprise evidence. Evidence is further distinguished from data by the fact that it contributes to discrimination among alternative end states. Data, while relevant, do not necessarily allow discrimination.

from the evidence. At their most basic level, these inferences depend on credibility (can it be believed), relevance (does the evidence bear on the issue), and inferential or probative force (how compelling is it in answering the questions raised by the issue). Unfortunately, no mass or body of evidence – in intelligence or anywhere else – comes with these three properties already established. Establishment of these properties to abet uncertainty reduction through inference occurs only through a process of argument, creative hypothesis generation, and the development of chains of reasoning.

Authenticity, accuracy, and reliability represent criteria for establishing the credibility of tangible evidence.[128] An analyst striving

---

128 "Tangible evidence" is a technical term describing *things* that bear relevance to an issue under scrutiny. It is contrasted with "testimonial evidence"

person, the analysis was faulty because somewhere along the line they limited their suspects (introduced bias) regardless of reason (access, family connections, angel–like qualities, etc.). Although it would take time, the investigators should conduct quantitative and qualitative analysis, make a decision tree (options open to a mole in a heavy security environment), and then play Devil's Advocate. In addition, analysis never reveals one "solution" or "smoking gun"; it leads to two or three "options" which can be investigated in detail.

The instructor, pleased that someone in the class knew what the "Analysis of Competing Hypotheses" was, revealed the answers of the real–life case study: after three years of investigating, the case officers had the wrong person due to incorrect information in old reports and limiting their suspect list. Instead of going back to the original source information, the officers read old reports that were unfortunately biased by Agency politics and external societal events (1950–60s). The real mole was discovered over a decade later; he was the son of a former Agency chief, well educated and well liked, but did not have access to the information. The individual "borrowed" interesting reports from friends who had access, covered his tracks, and continued spying against the U.S. for several years. Just as the authorities were about to arrest him, he was found dead in a hotel room from a reported suicide, but the cops could not figure out how he had two bullets in his chest and one in the back of his head. Miracle suicide.

What is the moral of the story? Conduct a thorough analysis right the first time and you can catch a mole anytime. I only hope the attending case officers got the message, especially from a non–gun toting NSA analyst.

who wishes to remain anonymous, email to the author, 9 March 2006.

to determine authenticity may ask, "Is the evidence what it seems to be?" In determining accuracy, the key question is whether the piece of evidence or the system that produced it has the resolution to reveal what the analyst believes the event or record should reveal. Assessing reliability involves determining whether different means of collection produce the same results.

If, on the other hand, the evidence is testimonial, different criteria apply. The first thing to be established is whether the source is being truthful. Truthfulness is not absolute. Rather, it is time- and context-dependent. A source may believe he is being truthful about an issue or may have legitimate reasons to be untruthful about that issue. In

---

– what people say about the issue.

another time and about another issue, these impediments to veracity may not exist for that source. Therefore, establishing the truthfulness of a source can pose a significant challenge to the analyst.

In an ideal situation, a review of evidentiary relevance causes an analyst to examine the likelihood of any potential answer to the problem or question – a hypothesis – with an eye to the modification of existing hypotheses or even the invention of new ones. In other words, an analyst might theorize that a certain bit of evidence will indicate that an individual or a group of individuals will engage in nefarious activity. Yet, if none of the evidence at hand bears on the issue, then the analyst may need to reconsider – or even reject – this evidence based on its lack of relevance. The analyst also should consider that the individual *may not* engage in the activity.

What is true about the future is also true about the present and the past. A lack of evidence relevant to an issue should prompt analysts to reassess their theories about the issue at hand. For example, an unnamed FBI investigator in the 2001 anthrax case noted, "[Reasoning] says that if you think a person is your guy, but you can't find anything to put him in the game, you've got to keep looking at others."[129] The failure of the FBI to implicate its principal suspect forced it to consider other explanations as to who sent the anthrax-laden letters in September 2001 to political leaders and media figures.

The analyst also is concerned with how strongly the evidence

_____

129 Allan Lengel and Guy Gugliotta, "Md. Pond Produces No Anthrax Microbes: FBI Sought Clues In Deadly Attacks," *Washington Post*, 1 August 2003, A03. Cited hereafter as *Washington Post*, "No Anthrax." While this is a law-enforcement example, it illustrates good critical questioning about an apparent lack of evidence. Criminal investigation and intelligence analysis similarly assess events and evidence with the goal of description, explanation, and interpretation. The principal difference is that intelligence analysis endeavors to do so *before* the event occurs – in other words, *to estimate*. It is worth noting that over two years after the pond was drained the case remains unsolved; the individual under suspicion at the time was never charged with the crime. The FBI was unable to link the evidence to the individual. See for example, Allan Lengel, "Little Progress In FBI Probe of Anthrax Attacks: Internal Report Compiled As Agents Hope for a Break," *Washington Post*, 16 September 2005, A01.

undermines or supports the particular hypotheses under examination – the probative force of the evidence. Certain evidence, coming from certain kinds of sources, persuades more strongly than does other evidence drawn from other sources. Tangible evidence might have greater probative force than testimonial evidence. Consider, for example, a hypothetical biological weapons issue. Traces of certain toxic substances found near an alleged biological weapons lab carry greater probative force than the testimonial denials of the government of the country in which the lab and the samples were found.

The "ideal" analyst also assesses the objectivity, observational sensitivity, and competence of sources. One question suitable for this assessment is how biases may have corrupted a source's objectivity. Did the source see or hear the evidence directly, and under what conditions did this occur? A reality check also is made at this point. Does it makes sense that a particular source claims to have been in a position to make the observation or have access to the source of information?

Another consideration involves denial and deception. In assessing the evidence, the analyst should ask, "What is the likelihood that I am being deceived? This question is surprisingly difficult to answer accurately. Given that anchoring biases and confirmation heuristics cause analysts to find what they seek to find, a denial and deception hypothesis is often easily proved.[130] Critical thinking challenges this by forcing an examination of alternative points of view. For intelligence analysts, proactive, focused and surreptitious collection of information about the often minimal disconfirming evidence pays rich dividends.[131] In this case, the question becomes, "What is the likelihood that I am *not* being deceived?" Thus engaged, really good intelligence analysts create valuable knowledge.

---

130 Author's notes, National Defense Intelligence College, Denial and Deception Advanced Studies Program, Spring 2005. The author is a National Intelligence Council-sponsored participant in the Foreign Denial and Deception Committee's Denial and Deception Advanced Study Program at the NDIC.

131 Ben-Israel, "Logic of the Estimate Process," 708–709.

Facilitating Evidentiary Assessment

The questions that need to be asked about each piece of evidence are the same as those employed in critical thinking. In making her evaluation of what constitutes evidence, the analyst repeatedly asks "why": "Why do I believe this information is relevant to the question at hand (either against or for) and therefore exists as evidence?" "Why do I believe the source to be credible?" Additional questions about the analyst's own thinking processes might arise, such as: "What are my biases and why do they lead me to think this way?"

For example, in assessing the intentions of former Iraqi dictator Saddam Hussein in light of the U.S. destruction of his intelligence headquarters in 1993, an analyst might ask whether Hussein's declarations not to retaliate against the United States were credible. A corollary question might be, "What does Saddam Hussein gain by denial and deception?" Based on Hussein's statement, a determination that additional evidence was needed would stimulate collection of similar statements from other episodes. By analyzing what Hussein did in those instances, the analyst might determine that he was usually untruthful. Therefore, this piece of evidence would be deemed to be of low credibility despite its probative force, and relevance to the determination whether Hussein would or would not retaliate.[132] In other words, Hussein's statement might reflect an ongoing deception campaign. To explore this hypothesis further, the analyst might seek to determine whether increases in Iraqi agent communications were relevant to the issue and whether additional collection of such broadcasts was warranted.[133]

In practice, these and similar questions can be answered quickly. Analysts often answer some of them unconsciously as they struggle

132 Heuer develops this scenario and evidence in an example of the analysis of competing hypotheses. See Heuer, *Psychology*, 101–102.

133 Heuer, *Psychology*, 101–102. For a recent detailed look at Saddam Hussein and deception see Kevin Woods, James Lacey, and Williamson Murray, "Saddam's Delusions: The View from the Inside," *Foreign Affairs* 85, no. 3 (May/June 2006). URL: <http://www.foreignaffairs.org/20060501faessay85301/kevin-woods-james-lacey-williamson-murray/sadda-s-delusions-the-view-from-the-inside.html>, last accessed 31 March 2006.

to meet short deadlines. However, as a function of not employing scientific methods or other structured and critical thinking techniques, their thinking is largely intuitive. Analysts choose to ignore how mindsets and assumptions impede their judgments. Conversely, critical thinking ensures that the reasoning process is a self-conscious one. By making the unconscious conscious, analysts reveal where they may be biased, helping ensure that questions they address are thoroughly and fairly considered.

> Each method of analysis uniquely interacts with the intelligence question; therefore, the method (or methods) selected can produce profoundly different results – affecting the analyst's arrival at the most accurate answer.

An analyst committed to critical thinking continually asks questions while developing the mass of evidence needed to assess an issue. Evidence arises from questions answered satisfactorily. Information for which the questions cannot satisfactorily be answered is excluded – but only after the analyst reflects on the process of evidence development. Consideration is owed to the question of how biases, and possibly active denial and deception by an adversary, have influenced the selection of both questions and answers. One way of revealing bias is by asking questions such as, "If the opposite outcome is actually true, what other evidence would I expect to see?"

The marshaling of evidence refers to a questioning process by which data and information are assessed and evidence is created. It may be done in solitary fashion, Socratically with a teammate, or collegially among Intelligence Community focus groups. It is a vital ingredient of productively imaginative intelligence analysis. Each question an analyst asks not only becomes a device for attracting existing evidence, but also generates new evidence not yet visible. Identifying new evidence increases the thoroughness by which the issue is evaluated and increases the probability that the correct solution has been discovered.

Embracing a Methodology

Once a relevant mass of evidence is established, the analyst evaluates which method or methods of analysis may best develop a solution to the issue. Differences among various analytic methodologies, techniques, and tools are not trivial.

In fact, comparing the results of different analysis methods can be a valid means of establishing the accuracy of the answer. If various means of analysis yield multiple results, a review by different analysts makes for the ideal environment for critical thinking to discuss and debate those results.[134]

Therefore, assessment of the available evidence includes redirecting thinking, soliciting feedback from other sources, appraising the quality of possible answers, and comparing initial goals with results. In so doing an analyst employs interpretive and evaluative skills to select the best mass of evidence to analyze.

Creating Better Inferences

Critical thinking aims to ensure that inferences are reasonable and evidence-based. Inference creation begins at the same time that analysis starts. As each piece, or the whole mass of evidence, is considered, inferences are made.[135] Resulting "chains" of inferences linking the evidence to the hypotheses under consideration are known as arguments. Chains of inferences converge – strengthening the argument – or diverge – weakening it. The self-reflective nature of critical thinking places a check on these inferences. The analyst asks, "Do my inferences flow from the evidence?" and, "Are my inferences logical given the evidence and other inferences I have made?"

Inferences lead to a search for additional evidence. In other words, based on inferences drawn from the evidence at hand, an analyst may infer that there are other sources of evidence to consider. For example, such reasoning was cited in the explanation of why

134 For a more detailed discussion of this and other means of countering biases, see Heuer, *Psychology*, 170–184; Irving Janis, *Groupthink: Psychological Studies of Policy Decisions and Fiascoes*, 2nd Edition (Boston, MA: Houghton Mifflin Company, 1982); and Scott Plous, *The Psychology of Judgment and Decision-making* (New York, NY: McGraw Hill, Inc., 1993).

135 Indeed, the analyst's acceptance – or rejection – of this evidence is a result of inferences: either the evidence is valid, credible, and relevant, or it is not.

the FBI investigated a pond in western Maryland during June 2003, searching for the source of the 2001 anthrax attacks. At the time, the FBI believed their primary suspect lived near the pond in question. In their search for additional evidence, they reasoned that the pond might be something in which evidence had been hidden. Thus, inference led the FBI to drain the pond to search for that evidence.[136]

The analyst self-consciously evaluates the thinking process and the biases that have affected it to reduce unproductive thinking and to consciously develop new ways of understanding the evidence at hand. This self-regulation also plays a role as the available evidence is considered. A means of accomplishing this within a collaborative setting is to seek the assistance of colleagues of diverse backgrounds. The underlying premise is that their biases differ sufficiently to enable productive and thorough analysis to occur.[137]

Producing Intelligence

Analysts who produce intelligence assessments and judgments have the opportunity to employ what Peter Facione considers the core cognitive skills of critical thinking: interpretation, analysis, evaluation, inference, explanation, and self-regulation.[138] Each of these competencies contributes to the integration of available evidence through a clear line of reasoning to the most probable answer.

Facione asserts that good critical thinkers can explain "what they think and how they arrived at that judgment."[139] By documenting the

---

136   *Washington Post*, "No Anthrax."

137   See Robert Callum, "The Case for Cultural Diversity in the Intelligence Community," *International Journal of Intelligence and Counter Intelligence* 14, no. 1, Spring 2001: 25–48.

138   Peter A. Facione, Critical Thinking: What It Is and Why It Counts (Milbrae, CA: California Academic Press, 1998, updated 2004), URL<http://www.insightassessment.com/>, last accessed 22 July 2005, 4. Cited hereafter as Facione, Critical Thinking.

139   Facione, *Critical Thinking*, 5.

reasoning process used to arrive at an answer, analysts move beyond merely "stating results [to] justifying procedures, and presenting arguments."[140] Questioning biases and mindsets encourages consideration of alternative possibilities that overcome what Josh Kerbel refers to as "single–outcome [analytic] trajectories."[141] Most importantly, analysts demonstrate a critical spirit – a reflection of character.[142]

Thus, critical thinking contributes to short-term analysis and assumes an essential role in longer-term analysis. Indeed, building a comprehensive picture of an issue or target requires critical thinking to determine which previous reports are included or excluded. "How do the parts contribute to the whole?" is one question the analyst asks. Another is, "How is the whole greater than the sum of its parts?" When previously published intelligence reports diverge, the critical thinking process helps the analyst ensure that the divergence is considered fairly and that the resulting intelligence does not merely satisfice.

140 Facione, *Critical Thinking,* 6.

141 Josh Kerbel, "Thinking Straight: Cognitive Bias in the US Debate about China," *Studies in Intelligence* 48 no. 3 (2004), URL: <http://cia.gov/csi/studies/vol48no3/index.html>, last accessed 22 February 2006.

142 Facione, *Critical Thinking,* 7. See also Moore and Krizan, "Intelligence Analysis," 9–11.

HOW CAN ANALYSTS BE TAUGHT
TO THINK CRITICALLY?

Many people would rather die than think – in fact, they do.

—Bertrand Russell

Critical Thinking Education
Outside the Intelligence Community

Critical thinking offers a framework for structured problem solving. Yet, despite a corpus of associated literature, critical thinking remains in its infancy as a discipline. It is still "largely misunderstood…existing more in stereotype than in substance, more in image than in reality."[143] As Bertrand Russell's humorous quip reminds us, critical thinking is not a habit acquired by just being alive.

Ideally, valuable skills and dispositions should be developed among prospective analysts before they join intelligence-producing corporations. Yet, observations by the author of newly hired intelligence analysts suggest this happens rarely if at all. This raises two questions, "What are the opportunities for prospective analysts to become critical thinkers before they are hired?" and often "Why do these opportunities not exist?"

Despite its importance, critical thinking is not widely taught in schools and universities. A mid-1990s California study on the role of critical thinking in the curricula of 38 public and 28 private universities concluded that the skill is "clearly an honorific phrase in the minds of most educators."[144] The study concluded that university

---

143   Richard W. Paul, "A Draft Statement of Principles," The National Council for Excellence in Critical Thinking, URL: <www.criticalthinking.org/ncect.html>, last accessed March 18, 2003. The reasons why critical thinking remains an undeveloped discipline while important, go beyond the scope of this essay and are not addressed.

144   Richard W. Paul, Linda Elder, and Ted Bartell, "Executive Summary,

faculty members "feel obliged to claim both familiarity with it and commitment to it in their teaching, despite the fact that...most have only a vague understanding of what it is and what is involved in bringing it successfully into instruction."[145] Indeed, the authors of the study found that while 89% of the faculty they interviewed "claimed critical thinking was the primary objective of their instruction," only 19% could define the term and only 9% were evidently using it on a daily basis in their instruction.[146] If the results of the California study are representative of the nation at large, they explain why prospective new hires – themselves college graduates – generally fail to exhibit skill in critical thinking at any level of proficiency.[147]

Informal conversations with recent hires at NSA support this premise. Although slightly fewer than half of these individuals indicate they have been exposed to critical thinking skills in college, most have been exposed only in one class and then only as an approach to learning the materials covered in that class. While not discouraged, respondents apparently were not encouraged to apply the skills to other subjects. Thus, a disposition to think critically is rarely fostered. Further, when asked to define critical thinking, most

Study of 38 Public Universities and 28 Private Universities To Determine Faculty Emphasis on Critical Thinking In Instruction," *California Teacher Preparation for Instruction in Critical Thinking: Research Findings and Policy Recommendations,* California Commission on Teacher Credentialing, Sacramento California, 1997 (Dillon, CA: Foundation for Critical Thinking, 1997), URL: <criticalthinking.org/schoolstudy. htm>, last accessed March 18, 2003. Cited hereafter as Paul, Elder, and Bartell, *Executive Summary.*

145 Paul, Elder, and Bartell, *Executive Summary.*

146 Richard W. Paul, Linda Elder, and Ted Bartell, *California Teacher Preparation for Instruction in Critical Thinking: Research Findings and Policy Recommendations California Commission on Teacher Credentialing,* Sacramento California, 1997 (Dillon, CA: Foundation for Critical Thinking, 1997), 18.

147 A recent but unscientific survey of several major eastern American universities' online catalogs shows the term "critical thinking" to be used widely in course descriptions. Further examination of some of those courses suggests that East Coast academics may share a similar lack of understanding about critical thinking. Although beyond the purview of this paper, it appears that there is sufficient evidence to warrant repeating the California survey on a national basis.

young analysts were unable to do so in any comprehensive fashion.[148] Finally, few employ any form of critical thinking in their analytic (or other) reasoning unless they have been trained to do so.

In fairness, it should be noted that critical thinking awareness, attitude, and skills varies from one academic discipline to another. For example, students of the physical sciences who employ the scientific method in a community setting probably have a greater inclination toward a basic form of critical thinking if only through osmosis.[149]

There are also some primary, secondary, and university education programs that have adopted a meta-cognitive critical thinking paradigm. Although the results of the impact of such programs are largely anecdotal, at least one study, conducted by Jennifer Reed as part of her dissertation found that students' critical thinking skills improved *after just one course.*[150] Faculty and administrators of these programs routinely attend the annual critical thinking conference sponsored by the Center for Critical Thinking where their results are shared. However, the approximately 500 people who attend this international event represent a small fraction of the educators in the United States.

The elements of scientific method – the formulation of hypotheses, collection of relevant data, testing and evaluation of hypotheses, and the logical derivation of conclusions – are matched step-by-step by

148   These conversations occur routinely as part of a training course the author teaches to newly hired intelligence and language analysts at NSA. When asked to complete the following statement, "In my opinion, critical thinking involves…" typical answers center on "thinking outside the box."

149   Francis J. Hughes, conversation with the author, Washington, DC: National Defense Intelligence College, 8 May 2003. Mr. Hughes is one of the few proponents and teachers of evidence-based inferential intelligence analysis, a means of analysis requiring critical thinking at every stage in the process.

150   Jennifer H. Reed, *Effect of a Model For Critical Thinking on Student Achievement In Primary Source Document Analysis And Interpretation, Argumentative Reasoning, Critical Thinking Dispositions, And History Content in a Community College History Course,* PhD Dissertation, College of Education, University of South Florida, December 1998, vii. URL: <http://www.criticalthinking.org/resources/JReed-Dissertation.pdf>, last accessed 6 May 2006.

critical thinking.[151] Given that most newly hired intelligence analysts – at least at NSA – are drawn from fields other than the physical sciences, one can expect that new hires lack adequate critical thinking skills. If NSA's newly hired intelligence analysts are representative of those being hired across the Intelligence Community then it is probable that few of the thousands of new hires arrive with adequate critical thinking skills.

Critical Thinking Education
Inside the Intelligence Community

That analysts need to develop critical thinking skills is recognized within the Intelligence Community. Heuer wrote in 1999, "[Traditionally], analysts at all levels devote little attention to improving how they think."[152] As a direct response to Heuer's criticism, the CIA's Sherman Kent School includes critical thinking as part of the curricula for training new analysts, and recently initiated a class in critical thinking.[153] New employees are encouraged to develop a disposition to think critically as they are taught the skills of intelligence analysis.

A similar approach is employed in courses on structured analysis methods at the National Defense Intelligence College (NDIC). Critical thinking is claimed as a feature of many NDIC courses. However, the emphasis in most courses is on topical or issue-related material, and only incidentally on the process of thinking. At present, the skill itself is largely not taught. Instead, students are expected to figure

---

151   Steven D. Schafersman, "An Introduction to Critical Thinking," January 1991, URL: <www.freeinquiry.com/critical-thinking.html>, last accessed 9 March 2006.

152   Richards J. Heuer, Jr., *Psychology of Intelligence Analysis* (Washington, DC: CIA Center for the Study of Intelligence, 1999), 173. Cited hereafter as Heuer, *Psychology*.

153   For a detailed account of how the faculty of the CIA's Sherman Kent School are working to improve their analysts' knowledge, skills, and abilities, see Stephen D. Marrin, "CIA's Kent School: Improving Training for New Analysts," *International Journal of Intelligence and Counter Intelligence* 16, no. 4 (Winter 2003–2004): 609–637.

it out on their own, encouraged by the thesis writing process. The college is aware of the importance of critical thinking and new core courses may include formal critical thinking instruction.

New NSA analysts are provided with an introduction to the solitary part of the skill (as discussed in figure 4) as part of their orientation. The agency's 40-hour follow-on program is the first Intelligence Community course to focus primarily on enhancing analysts' solitary and communal critical thinking skills. In addition to critical thinking skills, participants learn and apply, and then assess, the appropriateness of fourteen structured methods of analysis. The course has been taught to both U.S. and Allied personnel drawn from intelligence, counterintelligence, information assurance, and law enforcement communities.[154]

Training in critical thinking is offered to Defense Intelligence Agency (DIA) analysts using a variation of the NSA-developed course. Also, in 2005, DIA tested the "critical thinking skills" of a sample of its employees using the *Watson-Glaser Critical Thinking Appraisal*. The instrument claims to "measure abilities involved in critical thinking, including the abilities to define problems, select important information for the solution to problems, recognize stated and unstated assumption, formulate and select relevant and promising hypotheses, [and] draw valid conclusions and judge the validity of inferences."[155] The appraisal appears to confuse abilities with skills, although both do belong within the domain of analysis.[156] Finally, it appears that the test does not evaluate an individual's meta-cognitive skills in assessing and correcting the *process* of reasoning.

The increasing opportunities for enhancing critical thinking skills and dispositions reflect a recognition of the importance of critical

---

154 The syllabus from the course is in the Appendix.

155 Harcourt Assessment, Inc., *Local Norms Report, Watson-Glaser Critical Thinking Assessment*, Report prepared for the Defense Intelligence Agency, 2005, 2. Cited hereafter as Harcourt, *Watson–Glaser*.

156 Abilities and skills are easily differentiated. Individuals are born with certain abilities (and can improve them through training) but they *must* learn a skill. See for example, Moore and Krizan, "NSA."

thinking in intelligence analysis.[157] Evidence becomes intelligence through an "ordered thinking process [involving] careful judgments or judicious evaluations leading to defensible conclusions" – through critical thinking.[158] Former CIA analyst Morgan Jones asserts that methods for critical thinking and problem solving, if applied, can improve the quality of analysis and decisionmaking.[159]

Implications of Teaching Critical Thinking

Although Sherman Kent, Richards J. Heuer, Jr., and others have over the years addressed intelligence analysis and its relationship with critical thinking, recent presidential executive orders and legislative mandates are bringing a new emphasis to how the Intelligence Community can change analytic practices to achieve improved outcomes. Teaching analysts to be better critical thinkers may be seen as an easy way to satisfy these requirements. However, linkages between intelligence analysis and critical thinking remain poorly understood. Considerable confusion remains about what constitutes critical thinking and how it supports intelligence analysis.

A common excuse among analysts to defend their "non-use of such self-conscious processes is a lack of time."[160] Teaching critical thinking skills is of little value if analysts are not inclined to use them.[161] For those who are willing to think critically, various

157 The Director of National Intelligence, John D. Negroponte, in the Foreword of the initial *National Intelligence Strategy of the United States of America* (Washington, DC: Office of the DNI, October 2005), wrote that one of the three principal tasks for the reformed Intelligence Community is to "bring more depth and accuracy to intelligence analysis." See http://www.dni.gov/NISOctober2005. pdf.

158 Moore and Krizan, "Intelligence Analysis," 14.

159 Morgan D. Jones, *The Thinker's Toolkit: 14 Powerful Techniques for Problem Solving* (New York, NY: Random House, Inc, 1995), xi. Cited hereafter as Jones, *Thinker's Toolkit.*

160 Stephen Marrin, email to the author, December 8, 2003. The author has heard similar complaints from analysts at NSA and DIA.

161 Linda Elder, Alec Fisher, Diane Halpern, Gerald Nosich, Richard Paul, and others develop and publish the materials for – as well as teach – such courses.

instructional models offer complementary means of expanding and enhancing analysts' skills. For example, in an area studies class on Russia, students might be asked to evaluate and comment in depth on what different sources say about the influence of organized crime on the national government. Alternatively, critical thinking can be injected into the course as part of a problem-solving curriculum. Here students focus on *how* they think as they apply different strategies to each assignment, and then, ideally, transfer those enhanced skills to their day-to-day analysis. The use of realistic case studies makes classroom-acquired knowledge actionable. Self-reflective and group-reflective analyses of the process of reasoning keep the classes focused toward the working environment of analysts.

Such transformations involve behavior modification and as such take time. Participants engaged in such instruction cannot be expected to become critical thinkers in a one-day or even a week-long course. The instructors of the NSA course attempt over a period of 10 weeks to transform their students into critical thinkers. Some other Community efforts also provide instruction over an extended period. Even so, students leaving the course are still novices in this practice and can slip back to their old methods of reasoning. Becoming critical thinkers requires a change in behavior that extends long past the end of the formal instruction. There is no substitute for continued practice.

Finally, it serves critically thinking analysts poorly if their management and corporations are indisposed toward the application of the skills. It is well known that "engendering the desire to use [critical thinking] as a favored means of problem solving and decision making prepares the ground for teaching and learning the [critical thinking] skills."[162] Such encouragement can occur in the classroom but its effectiveness is limited unless the corporation encourages and welcomes strategies to employ critical thinking in the workplace.

However, there are few metrics for determining the effectiveness of these materials and courses and so their value remains undetermined. The fact that the books developed for, and used in, such courses remain in print (in successive editions) is an indicator that at least this approach is popular, if not effective.

162 Facione, "Disposition."

The best place for such encouragement is from senior and midlevel management. In order for this to occur, they too must be educated in the methods of, and reasons for, critical thinking.

Evaluating Teaching Models

Removing analysts from their work for education and training disrupts their primary mission of intelligence production. Spreading instruction over time provides a reasonable answer to this dilemma. Since improving critical thinking requires a high level of experiential, hands-on practice, an extended course offers students time to practice and apply what they are learning. This is the model used for the NSA course on critical thinking. Feedback from students indicates that once-a-week instruction works best. Mission is minimally disrupted and there is time to study and practice what is being taught. However, the long duration limits students' work-related travel and leave.

Experiential learning also requires that such classes be relatively small and that instructors be proficient. Without a large teaching staff, training a large workforce takes years. Since senior managers – and their strategic visions – change often, a long-term corporate commitment is crucial to success.[163]

Such a long-term commitment exists at the Sherman Kent School for Intelligence Analysis. The school itself grew out of a month-long course on analytic tradecraft developed by former Deputy Director for Intelligence Douglas J. MacEachin.[164] Beginning in 1996, the course was delivered to the entire analytic workforce. The school itself was established in 2000 and continues to evolve as both a training center and a center of best analytic practices.[165]

---

163 Alternately, a large staff can be created, trained, and assigned to teach an entire workforce. This was accomplished in a knowledge domain at NSA in the 1990s. If inducements and cultural change accompanied such a program, this approach might present certain advantages even if its costs are high. An analytic workforce could be transformed rapidly through such a "boot camp" approach.

164 Marrin, "Kent School," 615.

165 Marrin, "Kent School," 609.

Another means of critical thinking instruction is to create an interactive, computer-based or web-based course. This has the benefit of allowing as many analysts to attend as wish to do so. One or two instructors working full-time can answer students' questions. Exercises allow student self-assessment. However, this is presently an unsatisfactory model for critical thinking instruction. Learning to think critically requires Socratic interaction and the impersonal nature of web-based instruction discourages the practice even for the population of dedicated solitary learners. In the future, multi-player simulations and other games could be used to reinforce the lessons learned. However, these are not yet available.

Although computer- and web-based instruction can be accomplished at the analyst's desk, there are other reasons why this may not be a good idea. Analysts who remain in their offices are subject to interruptions. Further, course work is often relegated to the end of the workday, when analysts are tired and learning is impaired. Little learning occurs when taking a class is a chore. The current limitations of both classroom and computer- or web-based education suggest that experimentation with new means of instruction for critical thinking is needed.

Encouraging Analysts to Think Critically

Incorporating critical thinking into both orientation and basic analyst education and training is one way to help newly hired analysts develop their skills. Subsequently placing those analysts in offices where critical thinking is practiced is another way to encourage an analytic culture that fosters thinking critically. Through direct exposure to successful, experienced analysts, junior analysts' doubts about the employment of critical thinking techniques can be overcome.

"Skills pay" can be an inducement for analysts to learn and then employ critical thinking. Rewarding the acquisition, maintenance, and use of other special skills is common in government and industry. For example, linguists at NSA earn significant bonuses for achieving specific levels of foreign-language proficiency – an effective way to maintain critical language competencies within one intelligence agency's workforce. Given the high-level concern for the health of the intelligence analysis process, direct monetary incentives should be available for analysts to master new tools and demonstrate constructive analytical behaviors.

On the other hand, if an intelligence enterprise fails to recognize and reward the acquisition and application of analytic skills such as critical thinking, it sends a very clear message: the enterprise does not value those skills. Faced with such a message and a lack of inducements to excel, the best and brightest analysts may leave, especially from the more junior ranks – and midlevel employees with families and mortgages may "retire in place." Either outcome hurts mission-critical functions, and can be avoided. As a previous Director of NSA, Air Force Lieutenant General Kenneth A. Minihan, noted, "If we don't win the talent war, it doesn't matter what we invest in the infrastructure."[166] Recognizing and rewarding critical thinkers is one way to win that talent war – with the assumption that really good analysts are more likely to remain active within their intelligence agency workforces.

If an analyst adopts a congeries of skills that contributes to the mastery of critical thinking, and is compensated monetarily, that mastery needs to be certified. If a curriculum that drives the acquisition of those skills is in place, then an assessment of those skills can be administered in-house. Specific tests exist for the assessment of critical thinking, such as the "Thinking Skills Assessment Test."[167]

Persuading to Improve Analysis

Teaching critical thinking is but a first step toward improving analysis. Because analysts and managers have different needs and

---

166 LtGen Kenneth A. Minihan, USAF, Director, NSA, in Robert K. Ackerman, "Security Agency Transitions from Backer to Participant," *Signal* 53, no. 2 (October 1998), 23.

167 For more information, see http://tsa.ucles.org.uk/index.html, last accessed 15 March 2006.

time constraints, multiple versions of a course are needed to meet the needs of each group. Analysts and first-line supervisors may take an entire course, midlevel managers an abbreviated course, and senior managers an overview. This strategy already is employed at the CIA's Sherman Kent School where new employees spend 13 weeks learning analysis skills, techniques, and methods while supervisors, depending on their seniority, spend three days or one day becoming familiar with these same skills and methods. The analysts also have opportunities to apply new skills immediately as they perform four-week "internships" in various CIA offices.

Other CIA analysts, already in place, do not have the same opportunities to receive this training. Thus a two-tiered analyst population with more skilled junior analysts and more knowledgeable senior analysts is being created. Ideally, each will transfer skills and knowledge to the others. However, an alternate possibility is that it will generate distrust and animosity between the two groups. Older, more experienced analysts may resent the opportunities given to their newer counterparts. This issue is not trivial. Offering the wrong curriculum to the wrong groups of analysts and managers can destroy its effectiveness. Managers in the CIA and elsewhere can influence how the new analytic methods being taught will be adopted, as agencies respond to new legislative and executive mandates.

Will analysts embrace critical thinking as a means to improve their analysis? There are numerous observations of analysts' reluctance to adopt new paradigms.[168] This is true even when analysts are confronted with the fact that their conclusions were wrong. In referring to her work on the issue of Iraqi WMD, one CIA analyst told Senate investigators, "their 'bottom line' judgments would have remained the same."[169] Rob Johnston also found a similar reluctance to change opinions among the analysts he studied. He noted that

168 Stephen Marrin, "Homeland Security and the Analysis of Foreign Intelligence," Markle Foundation Task Force on National Security in the Information Age, 15 July 2002, URL: <www.markletaskforce.org /documents/ marrin_071502.pdf>, last accessed December 9, 2003, 9. Cited hereafter as Marrin, "Homeland Security."

169 SSCI, *Iraq*, 299.

although "analysts can change an opinion based on new information or by revisiting old information with a new hypothesis," they perceive a loss of trust and respect and a subsequent loss of "social capital, or power, within [their] group."[170]

Yet, a case can be made that analysts, and especially experienced analysts, will benefit the most from enhanced critical thinking skills training. These are the analysts who are in positions of technical leadership, who work the most difficult aspects of complex targets. There may be significant consequences if they fail to notice and make sense of an issue. On the other hand, the fact that many of these senior personnel will soon be eligible for retirement raises an important question: Does the corporation get added value from teaching analysts who will soon retire to think more critically in their analysis if they are predisposed not to do so? Maybe so. Heuer, while the head of CIA's Methods and Forecasting Division found that analysts, once persuaded to use new analytic methods, found them "interesting and well worth doing."[171]

Other intelligence analysts have adopted new analytic methods that add value to their analyses. In one example, NSA personnel involved in research and development adopted a means of matching target characteristics and their vulnerabilities with exploitation capabilities and their costs.[172] Such analyses helped ensure that appropriate resources were dedicated to collection and that such collection was better tailored to production analysts' needs. However, some research analysts initially refused to employ the model, claiming it took too much time even as it reduced the volumes of information

---

170 Johnston, *Analytic Culture*, 22.

171 Richards J. Heuer, Jr., *Adapting Academic Methods and Models to Governmental Needs: The CIA Experience* (Carlisle, PA: Strategic Studies Institute, U.S. Army War College, 31 July 1978), 5. Referenced in Marrin, "Homeland Security," 9.

172 In this context, a "target" refers to an entity – geographical, individual, or topical – in which the Intelligence Community has an interest.

they were required to examine.[173] Adoption of the analytic paradigm required appropriate persuasion.

One interesting means of self-persuasion may be analysts' frustration with the really hard problem. This frustration may lead analysts to try something new.[174] Such frustration occurs more often among experienced analysts. Years of attempting to make sense of overwhelming masses of information with inadequate analytic paradigms and technologies leaves some experienced analysts willing to grasp at anything that will improve how they work. On the other hand, newly hired analysts who have not yet experienced the frustration of inadequate paradigms for analysis may be resistant to adopting rigorous analytic paradigms such as that afforded by critical thinking.[175]

173 Multiple midlevel NSA analysts, interviews with the author, 1998–2005.

174 LT Robert D. Folker, USAF, email to the author, 9 December 2003. Cited hereafter as Folker, email, 9 December 2003.

175 Folker, email, 9 December 2003.

How does Critical Thinking Transform?

Transforming Intelligence Corporations

In order for an institution to change, all affected personnel, from the lowest to the highest, must first recognize that change is needed and is advantageous – both corporately and personally. As retired World Bank executive Stephen Denning argues, this is difficult to accomplish. Logically sound arguments do not sway employees. Instead, employees remain convinced that what they are doing is satisfactory.[176] Further, outsiders who attempt to induce change face opposition because employees presume that external consultants are arrogant in suggesting that things are not right, and that change is needed.

One way to effect change is through a "springboard story." This approach contrasts with past conventional – and largely unsuccessful – transformation efforts that relied on fixing the systems involved and were characterized by an overabundance of buzzwords:

> Enhance quality. Streamline procedures. Reform and flatten the organizational structure. Analyze things in terms of grids and charts. Develop plans in which individuals are programmed to operate like so many obedient computers. Hone our interpersonal mechanics and build skill inventories. Bring to our difficulties a fix-it attitude, as though our past errors can be easily corrected with straightforward explanations.[177]

---

176   For a discussion of Denning's philosophy about change, see Jeff de Cagna, "Making Change Happen: Steve Denning Tells the Story of Storytelling," Information Outlook, January 2001, 28–35, and Stephen Denning, *The Springboard: How Storytelling Ignites Action in Knowledge-Era Organizations* (Boston, MA: Butterworth-Heinemann, 2001). Cited hereafter as Denning, Springboard.

177   Denning, *Springboard*, xvii. In 23 years of Intelligence Community work, the author heard all of these phrases as slogans for various programs designed to "fix" analysis or the corporations involved. These associated corporate efforts to bring these goals about often had the opposite effect. In the process of "flattening

As Denning points out, these strategies fail to account for the messy and chaotic reality in which real organizations live and work, especially intelligence agencies which have the charter to engage honestly with "the other," or mission-related targets, outside of the bureaucracy in which they serve.[178]

The springboard story helps employees at all levels envision what is needed for the proposed transformation. Denning asserts that it "invites them to see analogies from their own backgrounds, their own contexts, their own fields of expertise."[179] He cautions that transformational stories are not a panacea – there are situations and circumstances in which they are not effective, such as when the change being proposed is a bad idea.[180] The key is finding the appropriate stories within the corporate culture.

One way to find these stories is to examine the best practices of intelligence analysis successes where critical thinking played a role. Just recounting a success is not enough. Listeners need to be able to identify and empathize with the scenario and its actors. The effective story is "about people who have lived [a] knowledge-sharing idea and how things happen in a real-life situation."[181] For example, conducting a trial or experiment on critical thinking within the intelligence analysis process, if it leads to certifiable, actionable success, *does* effectively persuade.

Learning from Early Adopters

Once a sustained number of early adopters openly apply systematic, critical thinking to hard analytic problems, the stage is set for a "tipping point" in the spread of structured methods across

---

the organization" at one intelligence agency, more hierarchical managerial layers were actually created!

178 Denning, *Springboard*, xvii.

179 Denning, *Springboard*, xix.

180 Denning, *Springboard*, xxi.

181 Denning, *Springboard*, 51.

analytic populations.[182] Stanley Feder recounts how a tipping point began to apply to a political analysis method at the CIA in the 1970s and 1980s. The method involved two estimative tools known as Factions and Policon that were used by the "Intelligence Directorate and the National Intelligence Council's Analysis Group to analyze scores of policy and instability issues in over 30 countries."[183] The reasons for the adoption of these tools remain the same: "Forecasts and analyses…have proved to be significantly more precise and detailed than traditional analyses."[184] Writing about the method in 1987, Feder predicted that its use would continue to expand.[185] The method is still in use 19 years after Feder's article was published. However, expanded use failed – perhaps because the tool was on a computer platform that ceased to be supported by the Agency. The recent transfer of the tool to a new suite of programs corresponds with observations that its use is once again expanding.[186]

Non-intelligence-related transformational stories can be applied in the Intelligence Community to facilitate the spread of new ways

---

182 Malcolm Gladwell, *The Tipping Point: How Little Things Can Make a Big Difference* (Boston, MA: Little Brown and Company, 2000), 15–29. Gladwell shows how "social epidemics" can infect a variety of domains.

183 Stanley Feder, "Factions and Policon: New Ways to Analyze Politics," in H. Bradford Westerfield, ed., *Inside CIA's Private World: Declassified Articles from the Agency's Internal Journal, 1955–1992* (New Haven, CT: Yale University Press, 1995), 275. Cited hereafter as Feder, "Factions and Policon."

184 Feder, "Factions and Policon," 292.

185 Feder, "Factions and Policon," 292. Feder was wrong about its sustained popular growth.

186 This story is not an isolated instance. In the author's experience, initial implementation and popularization are often followed by a gradually reduced user-base. Certain organizations find the tools useful and they tend to continue to use them even though any underlying technology may be obsolete. In the case of Factions and Policon, the tools were maintained on an aged Macintosh computer. They were updated in 2006 as part of the work of an intelligence research firm in New Mexico. The Factions tool was rewritten and included in Landscape Decision®, a suite of modeling and simulation tools developed under a research contract with the Department of Defense's Advanced Research and Development Activity (ARDA). The updated technology was reinserted into the tasking organization. Other technology transfers are pending.

of thinking. For example, two video commercial advertisements from the Electronic Data System (EDS) company resonate with the challenge of rebuilding intelligence analysis in the face of skeptics, and what it takes to be an intelligence analyst.[187] The two related commercials depict farcical situations based on two well-known clichés: "You've got to build it before you can fly it!" and "It's like herding cats; it can't be done!" In the former, a group of mechanics is building an airplane in mid-flight; while in the other, a group of cowboys has accomplished the impossible – they are herding cats across the Great Plains. EDS' depiction of its revolutionary design capabilities bears a message about corporate rebuilding and individual transformation. The message encourages managers and analysts to compare themselves and their situation to the people tasked with building an airplane at "60,000 feet," or with herding cats across a river.

Intelligence analysts and managers who have seen the videos have had little trouble drawing analogies with the corporate and personal transformations needed in the Intelligence Community. That the situations are humorous only adds to a viewer's buy-in – they are "hooked" before they realize it. Developing other stories that specifically apply to corporate transformation within the Intelligence Community and its various elements is a logical next step in encouraging analysts and managers to use and support critical thinking in analysis. If these stories can be drawn from recent analytic successes, their value can only increase.

The Costs and Benefits of Thinking Critically

Are intelligence failures inevitable if analysts lack critical thinking skills? Yes. However, critical thinking is not a panacea. Intelligence failures still can be expected. If no measure "will guarantee that accurate conclusions will be drawn from the incomplete and ambiguous information that intelligence analysts

---

187 See *Building Airplanes in Flight*, television advertisement produced for EDS by Fallon-McElligott, November 2000, videocassette; and *Herding Cats*, television advertisement produced for EDS by Fallon-McElligott, January 2000, videocassette.

typically work with...[and] occasional failures must be expected," why should the Intelligence Community invest in teaching its analytic workforce to think critically?[188] A brief review of the causes of failure clarifies the need for such an investment.

Intelligence failures occur in both systematic and functional domains. Systematic intelligence failures occur when producers fail to notice phenomena and the consumers of intelligence fail to heed warnings or even to notice that they are being warned. It may be that both consumers and producers are focused on other issues at the time. Alternatively, intelligence-based warning is not taken seriously at high official levels. In cases where collaboration among intelligence agencies might be critical, key evidence may not be recognized and shared.

All of these failings are illustrated in the "intelligence failure" to warn of the attacks of 11 September 2001 on the World Trade Center in New York and the Pentagon near Washington, DC. In the first place, the policy issue that was at the forefront − according to press at the time − was a national missile defense system, not the likelihood of a terrorist attack on the United States. Richard Clarke, the Clinton and then Bush administrations' terrorism "czar" observes that Bush administration officials were slow to recognize or consider the threats posed by Osama bin Laden.[189] Evidence passed by an FBI field agent about students learning to fly large aircraft with little regard for landing or takeoffs was not taken seriously at higher levels within the Bureau.[190] The Joint Congressional investigation into the attacks noted in its report that collaboration was lacking between agencies, especially between the law enforcement and strategic

188 Heuer, *Psychology*, 184.

189 "Clarke: Bush Didn't see Terrorism as 'Urgent,'" *CNN.com*, 19 May 2004, URL: <http://www.cnn.com /2004/ALLPOLITICS/03/24/911.commission/index.htm>, last accessed 9 March 2006.

190 Michael Elliott, "How the U.S. Missed the Clues," *CNN.com*, 20 May 2002, URL: < http://archives.cnn.com/2002/ALLPOLITICS/05/20/time.clues/index.html>, last accessed 9 March 2006.

intelligence agencies.[191] This was both a cultural and a physical phenomenon. Airport security breaches during the summer of 2001 may have been related, but based on assessments of the catastrophe, were not connected to the events.[192]

The same kinds of failings were identified by the Senate Select Committee on Intelligence in its assessment of the National Intelligence Estimate on Iraqi WMD. As has already been observed, analysts and their managers were focused on the results and not the process.[193]

Critical thinking can mitigate some common causes of failure and provide means by which they can be avoided in the future. Specifically, an intelligence process based on critical thinking offsets the following failures:

Analysts are Wrong. It is unrealistic to expect that analysts can always be correct. Regardless of the processes they employ, analysts make errors and fail. Anthropologist Rob Johnston defines *errors* as "factual inaccuracies in analysis resulting from poor or missing data." Conversely, intelligence *failures* are "systemic organizational surprise resulting from incorrect, missing, discarded, or inadequate hypotheses."[194] Critical thinking mitigates these by providing means to assess errors in reasoning as they occur and before they become

---

191   U.S. Congress, *Joint Inquiry into Intelligence Community Activities Before and After the Terrorist Attacks of September 11, 2001,* Report of the U.S. Senate Select Committee on Intelligence and U.S. House Permanent Select Committee On Intelligence, Together with Additional Views, Senate Report No. 107–351/House Report. No. 107–792, 107th Congress, 2nd Session, December 2002, xvi.

192   The author recalls that media reports of persons hopping over or otherwise improperly passing airport security checkpoints in and around Boston, New York, and Washington seemed to be higher than usual during the summer of 2001.

193   DNI Negroponte, in the *National Intelligence Strategy of the United States* (October 2005, 2) highlights the notion that the Community appropriately undertakes study of its internal processes, as well as of the quality of its products, by addressing both "enterprise" objectives as well as "mission" objectives.

194   Johnston, *Analytic Culture,* 6.

systemic failures. Such a meta-cognitive approach to the analytic process helps keep it under active review at the highest levels.

Policymakers Ignore Intelligence.[195] A critically thinking analytic population cannot directly affect what a policymaker can or will do — neither in fact, can a *non-critically thinking* analytic population. What critically thinking analysts can do, however, is present more effective assessments, perhaps leading policymakers to question their own assumptions on the issues. Additionally, thinking critically about how analysts interact with policymakers can identify ways to restructure the analysis dissemination process to involve policymakers more effectively. Such a process might also encourage them to adopt some of the attributes of critical thinking leading to (it may be presumed) more effective policy.[196]

Adversary Denies and Deceives. Critical thinking reduces the effects of adversarial denial and deception by leading analysts to consider alternative possibilities, to question biases and assumptions, to examine systematically the validity of evidence being considered, and to take seriously anomalies in the evidence.

Adversary is More Capable. In any adversarial system, there are winners and there are losers. While analysts can do everything possible to ensure their work is correct, they rarely work with all the evidence, and indeed may still be deceived. In such cases, they may come to wrong conclusions. Critical

---

195   There is a "classic" argument as to whether this is or is not an "intelligence" failure. In summary, the two sides condense as follows: On the one hand, intelligence should have been so persuasively presented as to compel the policymaker to pay attention. On the other hand, intelligence should not be telling the policymaker what to do. The argument goes all the way to the roots of the post-World War II strategic intelligence system currently in place. Former CIA analyst Jack Davis summarizes the issue in "The Kent-Kendall Debate of 1949," *Studies in Intelligence* 35, no. 2 (Summer 1991): 37–50.

196   Cooper, email to the author, 31 March 2006. Cited hereafter as Cooper, email, 31 March 2006.

thinking, however, by providing structure and oversight to their reasoning, provides an audit trail. In this case, the means by which the analytic conclusions were reached can be subsequently reviewed, errors and deceptions revealed, and steps taken to improve the process so that the failure is not repeated. Indeed, because of its focus on the process, critical thinking becomes a powerful tool for evaluating and enhancing analytical reasoning.

Investment in critical thinking as part of the analysis process minimizes the likelihood of specific failures. With critical thinking essential to so many parts of the intelligence production process, enhancing it increases the likelihood of intelligence success.[197] With the cost of failure catastrophically high, the Intelligence Community is well advised to improve the likelihood of intelligence success, including improving critical thinking. As diplomat Richard Holbrooke opined in 2003, "intelligence is...indispensable. And its greatest successes are preventative."[198]

There are other reasons why systemic intelligence failures occur. Jeffrey Cooper considers ten pathologies, summarized in table 6, that impede successful analysis at both the individual and corporate levels. Cooper specifically believes that given the

[emphasis] on the systemic nature of the pathologies that afflict intelligence analysis, structured analytic methods

---

197 One metric for intelligence is decreasing intelligence failures. In this case, fewer failures could be considered as "improving intelligence." But the reasons for the prevention of the failures need to be considered. The reduced number of failures could be due to a critically thinking workforce. Or it could be due to coincidences. Although a pointed discussion of metrics for intelligence is beyond the scope of this paper, recent articles explore the issue of intelligence metrics. See, for example, David T. Moore, Lisa Krizan, and Elizabeth J. Moore, "Evaluating Intelligence: A Competency-Based Model," *International Journal of Intelligence and Counterintelligence* 18, no. 2 (Summer 2005): 204–220.

198 Richard Holbrooke, in Judith Miller, "A Battle of Words Over War Intelligence," *New York Times*, online edition, 22 November 2003, URL: <www.nytimes.com/2003/11/22/arts/22INTE.html>, last accessed November 28, 2003.

Cooper's Analytic Pathology	Description
Inefficient "Account" Structure	Work is subdivided into accounts with ownership; provides basis for accountability; ownership inhibits sharing, cooperation, and collaboration; encourages "stovepiping" in collection disciplines.
Evidence-Based Scientism	Descriptive and explanatory intelligence support current policy and military operations; less support for anticipatory intelligence; analysis needs to be "augmented and leavened with intuition, curiosity, and a thirst for discovery – all essential elements of good science."
Tyranny of Current Intelligence	Response to customers' current concerns; support to current, ongoing military operations; little long-term research.
Over-Emphasis on Production	Databases need filling; scheduled reports and assessments must be produced on time; metrics for success measure data collected and processed; number of reports issued used to determine and justify resources allocated.
Over-Reliance on Previous Judgments	Previous reports presumed to be authoritative; previous reports combined to form new judgments; agreed-upon positions retained despite newer contradictory evidence.

Table 6: Cooper's Analytic Pathologies

Source: Summarized from Cooper, *Pathologies*, 30–39.

become a first line of defense in preventing the networks of errors from developing – they are like "ripstops" that keep problems from propagating into wider "error-inducing systems," in [Charles] Perrow's terms.[199]

---

199 Jeffrey Cooper, email to the author, 31 March 2006. Cooper refers to Charles Perrow, *Normal Accidents: Living with High-Risk Technologies* (Princeton, NJ: Princeton University Press, 1999).

Cooper's Analytic Pathology	Description
Neglect of Research	Short–term taskings prevent longer–term research; reward structure favors current reporting, not longer term work; stunts development of deep target expertise.
Neglect of Anticipatory Intelligence	"Information Revolution" leaves intelligence competing with journalism and Internet for policymakers' attention; lack of predictive intelligence against new emerging threats ensures continuing failures to warn.
Loss of "Keystone Species" and "Intellectual Middleware"	Periodic reductions in force skew analyst demographics; "Keystone Species" (journeymen analysts) lacking; journeymen do bulk of professional maintenance; essential for knowledge retention and transfer to apprentices; maintain "intellectual Middleware" or deep understanding of analytic domains and processes.
Lack of Analytic Tools and Methods of Validation	Available and proposed tools not formally validated for accuracy and usefulness; focus on results, not processes, to determine success.
Hindrances of Security Mindset	Security procedures impede multi–source analysis; protection of sources and methods more important than "effective exploitation and cross–fertilization;" artificial and outdated mission distinctions prevent collaboration.

Critical thinking combats this by enhancing the processes by which decisions are made and by which such processes are reviewed. This paper focuses primarily on *individual experience*, and of course, intelligence corporations are made up of individuals. If a sufficient number of intelligence professionals are thinking critically, it is likely they will transform their corporations, if only through the sheer attrition of non-critically thinking managers and leaders who are retiring from the work force. It should be observed that an Intelligence Community enterprise-wide emphasis on developing critical thinking skills at all levels would speed the process.

Validation

A critically thinking Intelligence Community remains essential for effective intelligence reform. Steven Rieber and Neil Thomason advance this argument in their recent article. The authors assert that "the opinions of experts regarding which methods [of analysis] work may be misleading or seriously wrong."[200] Unfortunately, as the authors show, past (and present) efforts at intelligence reform rely on expert intuitive judgments. However, "[examples] from a wide range of fields show that expert opinion about which methods work are often [not only] dead wrong…but also are generally not self-correcting."[201] Further support of Rieber's thesis is seen in devil's advocacy – not as theoretically applicable but as practiced. They cite Irving Janis who, quoting a Stanford political scientist, notes that "instead of stirring up much-needed turbulence among the members of a policymaking group, [devil's advocacy] may create 'the comforting feeling that they have considered all sides of the issue.'"[202]

To mitigate this and similar analysis-improvement fallacies, Rieber and Thomason argue that improvements in analysis and any proposed methods of judgment and decision-making require validation through scientific study. They note, for example, that research reveals "[a] certain cognitive style, marked by an open-mindedness and skepticism toward grand theories, is associated with

---

200 Rieber and Thomason, "Creation of a National Institute for Analytic Methods," 71.

201 Rieber and Thomason, "Creation of a National Institute for Analytic Methods," 72.

202 Irving L. Janis, *Groupthink: Psychological Studies of Policy Decisions and Fiascoes*, 2nd edition. (Boston, MA: Houghton Mifflin and Company, 1982), 268. Referenced in Rieber and Thomason, "Creation of a National Institute for Analytic Methods," 73.

substantially better judgments about international affairs."[203] As the present paper has argued, such attitudes are found in critical thinkers. Scientific study of this and other methods will determine when and how they are appropriate. Critical thinking also supports Rieber and Thomason's call for a "National Institute for Analytic Methods" by providing an overarching structure to champion open-mindedness and skepticism in the study of which methods are appropriate for intelligence analysis. Only then, they argue, will real intelligence reform and improvement occur.

Rieber and Thomason's proposed institute could determine which strategies are most effective at disposing analysts and their corporations to employ critical thinking. Research evidence indicates that simply teaching critical thinking (or for that matter, structured analytic) skills is insufficient. People will not adopt the strategies unless motivated to do so. As noted here, springboard stories are one means of implanting a positive disposition toward critical thinking. Other means certainly also exist. A desirable objective of research in the proposed National Institute for Analytic Methods would be to discover and assess what might motivate analysts most effectively toward thinking critically.

---

203   Rieber and Thomason, "Creation of a National Institute for Analytic Methods," 74.

WHAT OTHER POINTS OF VIEW EXIST?

A recent best-selling book advances the comfortable idea that conscious reasoning may not confer advantage to the reasoner.[204] Recent research suggests that whereas simple choices may benefit from conscious thought, complex issues are best left to unconscious thought, or "deliberation-without-attention."[205] The explanation of this finding is that in conscious thinking, people face a severe limit on the number of factors that they can effectively consider simultaneously and, second, that in conscious thought people "inflate the importance of some attributes at the expense of others."[206] The authors base this finding on four experiments with subjects who were asked to indicate their preference for various consumer items. The experiments involved differing levels of complexity in terms of factors to be taken into consideration. They ultimately suggest that:

> [there] is no *a priori* reason to assume that the deliberation-without-attention effect does not generalize to other types of choices – political, managerial or otherwise. In such cases, it should benefit the individual to think consciously about simple matters and to delegate thinking about more complex matters to the unconscious.[207]

It appears true that the human capacity to weigh evidence *consciously* is limited to approximately seven factors.[208] But this seven-

---

204 Malcolm Gladwell, *Blink: The Power of Thinking Without Thinking* (New York, NY: Little Brown and Company, 2005). Gladwell argues that thinking does not require detailed assessment of information. Instead, rapid cognitive responses are adequate for decisionmaking.

205 Ap Dijksterhuis, Martin W. Bos, Loran F. Nordgren, and Rick B. von Baren, "On Making the Right Choice: The Deliberation-Without-Attention Effect," *Science* 311, no. 5763 (17 February 2006), 1005. Cited hereafter as Dijksterhuis, "Deliberation-Without-Attention."

206 Dijksterhuis, "Deliberation-Without-Attention," 1005.

207 Dijksterhuis, "Deliberation-Without-Attention," 1005.

208 George A. Miller. "The Magical Number Seven, Plus or Minus Two," *The Psychological Review* 63 (1956), 87. The paper is available online: URL: < http://psychclassics.yorku.ca/Miller/>, last accessed 14 March 2006.

item limit is easily extended: people can hierarchically consider multiple sets of seven items.[209] Employing structured methods of reasoning also extends this capacity. In this context, critical thinking is at once both a structuring method and a means of assessing and monitoring the processes of selecting and using other structured methods. Additionally, "deliberation-without-attention" as applied to consumer choices in the study noted above was measuring *preferences*. Preferences change from person to person – different people conclude differently about oven mitts and cars – as the variety of these products on the market, in kitchens, or on the roads makes clear.[210]

Intelligence analysis is not about preferences; it is about best answers in ambiguous situations with high-stakes implications and consequences. As recent intelligence failures make clear, without forced consideration of alternatives, results are biased. Structured reasoning methods such as Analysis of Competing Hypotheses (ACH) develop these alternatives, allow for multiple factors to be considered fairly, and extend analyst capacities to assess complex situations as accurately as possible.

Intuition is what both Dijksterhuis and Gladwell consider in their respective works. However, exactly *what is intuition?* Rather than just appearing from nowhere, intuition is "almost always informed by experience and hard knowledge won by reasoning things out."[211] As Michael LeGault notes,

> good decisions [are] a nuanced and interwoven mental process involving bits of emotion, observation, intuition, and critical thinking....The essential background to all this is a solid base of knowledge...The broader the base, the more likely all the parts will fit together.[212]

---

209 William Reynolds, conversation with the author, 14 March 2006.

210 Oven mitts and cars are two of the categories for which Dijksterhuis and his colleagues tested.

211 LeGault, *Think*, 12.

212 LeGault, *Think*, 12.

Uninformed "intuitive thinking" contributes to intelligence failures because it fails to reflect on presuppositions. Such unexamined biases and mindsets contributed to the Cuban missile intelligence failure described above. Heuer's outline of the specific biases and mindsets that impede effective analysis is reinforced by the findings of others.[213] For example, Merom, writing about the Cuban crisis, concludes that intelligence failures occur due to a "lack of commitment to fundamental principles of investigation and analysis."[214] Although intuition or "thin slicing" may be appropriate in some domains, in intelligence analysis it appears to be associated with cognitive impediments that cause costly intelligence failures.[215]

However, as Rieber and Thomason note, testing needs to be conducted to determine which methods do work best in which situations in intelligence analysis.[216] Their work ought to go further, developing and modifying methods to overcome the very limitations they identify. For example, investigators have found that ACH suffers from confirmation bias.[217] The present author notes that this may be because non-confirmatory reasoning is so difficult for people to do.[218]

---

213 See for example, Scott Plous, *The Psychology of Judgment and Decision-making* (New York, NY: McGraw Hill, Inc., 1993); Thomas Gilovich, Dale Griffin, and Daniel Kahneman, Eds. *Heuristics and Biases: The Psychology of Intuitive Judgment* (Cambridge, UK: Cambridge University Press, 2002); and Daniel Kahneman, Paul Slovic, and Amos Tversky, eds. *Judgment under Uncertainty: Heuristics and Biases* (Cambridge, UK: Cambridge University Press, 1982).

214 Merom, "Estimate," 49.

215 Gladwell introduces the notion of "thin slicing" as a reasoning strategy in *Blink*.

216 Rieber and Thomason, "Creation of a National Institute for Analytic Methods," 76.

217 Brant A. Cheikes, Mark J. Brown, Paul E. Lehner, and Leonard Adelman, *Confirmation Bias in Complex Analyses*, Mitre Technical Report MTR 04B0000017 (Bedford, MA: Center for Integrated Intelligence Systems, October 2004).

218 The author teaches Analysis of Competing Hypotheses to both new and experienced analysts at the National Security Agency. He notes that holding a non-confirmatory attitude – which ACH, as developed by Heuer, requires – is

– 88 –

Finally, it may be a fallacy that conscious and unconscious reasoning are truly separate. Instead, Morgan Jones (citing work by Richard Restak) asserts that "the unconscious has a governing role in much that we consciously think and do."[219] This means that analysts commit a variety of "analytic sins," including focusing on the initially favored solution – which is also often the first satisfactory solution considered.[220] Part of the problem seems to arise from confusion about "'discussing/thinking hard' about a problem and 'analyzing' it, when the two activities are not at all the same."[221] Ultimately, the unconscious or instinctive approach to reasoning seems to "remain closed to alternatives."[222] This is an unsatisfactory model for intelligence analysis where alternatives *must* be considered.

---

extremely difficult for people to do. Since the method has value, a means of mitigating this difficulty is worth developing.

219 Jones, *Thinker's Toolkit*, 10. Jones bases his assertions and argument on the work of Richard Restak, *The Brain has a Mind of Its Own* (New York, NY: Harmony Books, 1991).

220 Jones, *Thinker's Toolkit*, 11.

221 Jones, *Thinker's Toolkit*, 11.

222 Jones, *Thinker's Toolkit*, 12.

WHAT DOES THE FUTURE HOLD?

Looking ahead, new paradigms for analysis become necessary in light of the many changes occurring across the globe. Rapidly emerging twenty-first century issues and challenges stress both infrastructures and sensemaking enterprises. The changes needed to maintain an edge against adversaries becomes clear as one considers what it is that analysts do, and how and when, as table 7 illustrates.

Gregory Treverton's observations about the evolution of intelligence sensemaking and the organizations that comprise the national intelligence enterprise suggest that current "reform" efforts are merely the first steps in a much lager – and fundamental – transformation. A careful, considered examination of what intelligence must accomplish and how this can be best achieved may ensure that the goals Treverton identifies as necessary for the future are met – and met sooner rather than later. Here again critical thinking has much to offer. By encouraging discussion of the alternatives and their advantages and disadvantages, and by examining analogous cases, critical thinkers aid the transformation. Questioning of assumptions about the roles of intelligence, its activity, and organization will reveal which long-held beliefs need retirement.

Further, technology efforts in support of analysis, such as those being developed through the efforts of the ARDA – and other – advanced technology efforts presume that analysts think critically. For instance, by focusing "analytic attention on the most critical information found within massive data,"[223] some research projects seek to uncover otherwise unknown information that indicates the potential for strategic surprise.[224] These projects seek to build

---

223 Critical information is that which is *essential* for analysts to make sense of what their targets are going to do. Often it is buried in massive amounts of "noise."

224 Advanced Research and Development Activity, *Broad Agency Announcement for the Novel Intelligence from Massive Data (NIMD) R&D Program*, NMA401–02–BAA–0004, 7 JUNE 2002, 1.

partnerships between analysts and technology applications.[225] In one case, a research firm has developed technology that enables analysts to generate and validate novel hypotheses, distill complex systems into digestible elements, create effective narratives, and inspire creative thinking.[226] Other examples are illustrated in the adjacent text box. Follow-on research efforts such as the Collaboration and Analyst/System Effectiveness (CASE) effort will develop these efforts further.[227] The intelligence workforce these ARDA-supported efforts presuppose is being hired and trained now.

The future also holds opportunities for further developing models of reasoning in intelligence. Exactly how analogy and critical thinking interact, the roles of creative thinking, the roles of intuition, and specific strategies for bias mitigation are all areas warranting further research. Formal validation of how critical thinking improves intelligence reasoning is another research topic. Rieber and Thomason's proposed National Institute of Analytic Methods is an obvious venue for such research. Additionally, the ARDA advanced questioning and answering research program, AQUAINT, as well as other ARDA programs dealing with predictive analysis, prior and tacit knowledge, and hypothesis generation offer other domains in which such research could occur.[228] Such research is of both intrinsic value and necessary for developing new means

---

225   The five areas on which the NIMD effort focused were modeling analysts and how they work; analysts' prior and tacit knowledge; creating, representing, and tracking multiple scenarios, hypotheses, and/or strategies; massive data management and analysis; and the means by which analysts interact with technology. The author represented his agency in evaluating and mentoring the efforts of the researchers.

226   The author is a technical mentor of this firm's work.

227   For more information, see "Collaboration and Analyst/System Effectiveness (CASE)," AFRL Directorate: IFED BAA 06–02–IFKA, 28 October 2005, URL: <http://www.rl.af.mil/div/IFK/baa/>, last accessed 11 March 2006.

228   Advanced Research and Development Activity (ARDA), "Preliminary Solicitation Information for Advanced QUestion & Answering for INTelligence (AQUAINT)," URL: <http://www.digitalgovernment.org /library/library/pdf/preliminary_information.pdf>, last accessed 26 March 2006.

Issue	1970s and 1980s
Focus of Analysis	Continuing large, well-defined issues and adversaries
	Space for longer-term thinking
Organization and Workflow	Large, centrally organized and managed
	Hierarchical
	Institutional and operational memory mostly in analysts heads
	Time pressure persistent but low intensity (mostly)
Sources and Methods	Dominated by secret sources
	Analysts are separated from collectors
	Analysts mostly passive recipients of information
	Analysis focuses on previous patterns
	Analysts operate on basis of own experience and biases
Analysts' Characteristics	Many analysts are deep specialists
	Analysts mostly work alone or in small groups
	Key analytic choices with analysts

Table 7: Analysis: Past, Present and Future

Source: Developed by Gregory F. Treverton with input from the author.

1990s and 2000s	Future
Emergence of complex, rapidly shifting issues and adversaries	Complex, rapidly shifting issues and adversaries and large, well-defined issues and adversaries
Bias toward current intelligence	Both immediate question–answering and deeper analysis
Large, centrally organized and managed	Tailored to rapidly adapt to shifting foci
Still hierarchical, though problem-oriented "centers" added	Flat, problem-centric networks
Institutional and operational memory mostly in analysts heads	Technology helps to notice what analysts are watching and asking
Time pressure drives toward premature closure	Technology allows memory even of hypotheses, data rejected by analysts
Broader range of sources, but secrets still primary	Draws on a wide variety of sources, open and secret
Analysts are also their own collectors	Analysts are their own collectors
Limited searching of available data	Much more aggressive searching and reaching for data…both classified and unclassified
Same, though growing interest in new methods and tools for shaping, remembering, and examining hypotheses	Formative pattern recognition and data mining capabilities searches for out of the ordinary
Limited use of formal method and technology	Wide use of method and technology – from aggregating expert views to searching, data mining, pattern recognition
Many, perhaps most, analysts are generalists	Mix of generalists and deep specialists, both technical and political
Analysts mostly work alone or in small groups	Analysts work in larger virtual networks
Key analytic choices with analysts	Key analytic choices with analysts

Email exchanges 17–18 May 2006.

of improving intelligence analysis. Knowing the details of how analysts reason and how they might reason more effectively guides managers to understand where educational and training efforts can be most valuable.

TECHNOLOGICAL ADVANCES IN CRITICAL THINKING

One ARDA research team has created a technological system employing an automated critical thinking-based model that provides an overarching control structure for analytic reasoning. It includes both model generation (for counter–examples) and more traditional argument building. The system's creators assert – based on preliminary testing – that analysts employing the system are faster and more accurate problem solvers.

Suppose an analyst develops an argument in the course of using this system, that confirms that Saddam Hussein has WMD and an argument that confirms that Saddam does not have WMD. Working both sides of this issue, this analyst will make inferences from evidence and link them with other evidence-derived inferences. She will not imagine a situation in which all her evidence is true, but her hypothesis is not. For example, the evidence might include communications from which she infers that those communicating – including Saddam's scientists – believe they have WMD. Using the system, she also would be led to consider that the scientists might have wanted to deceive Saddam into believing that they were further along than they were. The generation of this alternative model can only arise through a mechanism that conducts the analyst away from the comfortable, inductive, confirmation path associated with the initial hypothesis.

CONCLUSION

> Never before in our peacetime history have the stakes of
> foreign policy been higher.
>
> —Sherman Kent, 1949

This paper posed the intriguing question: "How can intelligence
analysts be 'really good'"? Critical thinking, if conceived and
employed by intelligence analysts as suggested here, appears capable
of leading analysts to adopt personal habits of thought appropriate
to the resolution of hard intelligence problems. The idea that
intelligence analysts are expected to bring to the table a capability to
draw reasoned and actionable conclusions from scant and conflicting
information distinguishes their charge from that of their academic
brethren. Thus, intelligence analysts in government or other applied
work environments may deserve the lavish budgets and technological
capabilities they often enjoy.

To earn their high level of resource support, analysts can take
advantage of a capability to redirect unique intelligence collection
capabilities. In doing so, they are perfectly positioned to apply critical
thinking methods to the hard problems. They can, for example,
order up special collection against targets that exhibit even fleeting
evidence that convincingly disconfirms one or more alternative
hypotheses about an impending threat. This is the nub of Ben-
Israel's argument for a "logical" approach to intelligence analysis
for national security, and is an approach no doubt under-used by
those who do not systematically think about threats in the manner
developed in this paper.

Although most of the specific threats have changed since Sherman
Kent first wrote in 1949, his epigraph remains as true today as it
was then: the survival and prosperity of the United States remain at
stake; they depend on effective, informed foreign policy.[229] Critical
thinking brings with it an indispensable capability to inform a rational

---

229 Kent, *Strategic Intelligence*, ix.

foreign policy. "Really good analysts" are those who think critically about the issues they work and the problems they solve; they bring structured thought to the foreign policy realm.

NSA's Critical Thinking and Structured Analysis Class Syllabus[230]

Background

Twenty-first Century intelligence issues involve uncertainty, mysteries, and risk. This differs from the 20th Century paradigms of security, secrets, and prevention. Analysis of current complex issues requires of its practitioners novel approaches including a productively imaginative process of inquiry. Questions an analyst asks not only serve as devices for attracting existing evidence, but also as devices for generating new evidence not presently considered. In this way, analysts more thoroughly examine complex issues and, aided by technology, are more likely to create novel intelligence and prevent strategic surprise.

However, such reasoning is at odds with how people – all people, including intelligence analysts – naturally think. Instead, people seek to confirm the first answer to a problem they discover, selectively using evidence to support that position *even when there is compelling evidence that an alternative hypothesis may actually be the correct one.* That people routinely fall prey to such poor thinking is well documented. Indeed, most commercial advertisers strive to take advantage of this. So do adversaries. One element of most intelligence failures includes poor thinking on the part of analysts— poor thinking of which adversaries have taken advantage. So how can analysts avoid such thinking?

One solution is to teach intelligence analysts to think critically.

---

[230] This syllabus has been developed and refined by the author through several years of teaching critical thinking at the National Security Agency's National Cryptologic School. An early version of the course bore similarity to one developed by (then) MSGT Robert D. Folker, while a student at the (now) National Defense Intelligence College. Folker's course focused on the methods of analysis, not on the overarching critical thinking. His course (as written) is not taught at the college.

Critical thinking provides structure to the reasoning process that identifies for analysts where they are likely to go astray. It offers a means for self-reflective reasoning that leads to improved thinking. If such thinking is aided by structured analytic techniques, then analysts will (and do) improve how they resolve issues with which they are confronted. The quality of their work improves.

This critical thinking and analytic problem-solving course offers participants a chance to learn a paradigm for critical thinking and critically explore 14 different structured methods of analysis. Texts by critical thinking experts Richard Paul and Linda Elder, and structured analysis experts Morgan Jones and Richards Heuer, as well as materials developed by the instructor, teach the concepts and techniques. Classroom problems as well as operational examples (introduced and developed by the students from their own work) reinforce and help transfer what is learned into the operational environment. A final project developed by student teams completes the formal requirements.

Learning to think critically and to solve problems in a structured manner requires active participation. The class requires 40 hours of classroom time, consisting of ten sessions of four hours each. The method of instruction is Socratic, demanding active classroom participation. Participants also can expect homework, requiring both office and non-office time. Participants will prepare reading summaries for each class session, and develop one (or more) operational examples of at least one structured analytic method. Finally, participants work together on teams to complete classroom assignments and a final project dealing with an operational issue (employing at least five structured analytic methods).

Administration:

Enrollment: Up to 21 Students.
Class Date/Time/Duration: One 4-hour class per day for 10 weeks.
Class Location: _____.
Homework: Yes, but hopefully not too odious. Operational examples are required. A team project is due at the end of the course.

Texts:

Elder, Linda, and Richard Paul. *The Foundations of Analytic Thinking: How to Take Thinking Apart and What to Look for When You Do* (Dillon Beach, CA: Foundation for Critical Thinking, 2003).

Heuer, Richards J., Jr. *The Psychology of Intelligence Analysis* (Washington, DC: Center for the Study of Intelligence, 1999), URL: <http://cia.gov/csi/books/19104/index.html>, last accessed 15 March 2006.

Jones, Morgan D. *The Thinker's Toolkit: Fourteen Skills for Making Smarter Decisions* in *Business and in Life* (New York, NY: Crown Publishing Group, 1997).

Several handouts (TBD)

Objectives:

The overall objective of the class is to enable you to critically think about analysis and what analysts are tasked to analyze. A second objective is to provide you with a set of analytic tools that are useful to your analysis. At the end of the class you will be equipped with a set of analytic skills and will have honed your critical thinking skills, allowing you to better function in the workplace. Specifically, the course objectives are as follows:

Upon completion of this course you will be able to:
- Use critical thinking techniques to provide structure to your analytic reasoning.
- Identify, describe, and employ 14 methods for structured reasoning.
- Demonstrate critical thinking proficiency through lecture, classroom participation, and weekly homework assignments.
- Complete a final class assignment using a minimum of five structured analytic methods presented in this course.
- Apply knowledge of critical thinking by using a set of analytic tools designed to hone your skills as an analyst.

In other words, at the end of this 10-week-long class, you will have
- Learned to critically analyze intelligence-associated data, information, and evidence.
- Honed your critical thinking skills.
- Built a "toolbox" of analytic and problem-solving methods.
- Become better analysts.

For example, when you approach a problem you will be able to
- Discover the true problem by restating and considering alternative outcomes.
- Have a variety of methods by which you can organize and make sense of the relevant evidence.

Formal Requirements:

Written summaries of readings. (No more than one page per chapter assigned.) The summaries should answer *exactly* the questions on page five of the syllabus. The summaries should also include answers to the exercises in Morgan Jones' book. The summaries will be typed unless prior arrangements have been made with the instructor. In-class discussions will draw heavily on the readings.

Problems from the work environment (Operational Exemplars). As we study the elements of reasoning and the methods of problem solving, we need operational examples against which to apply/illustrate what we are learning. You will be responsible for providing at least one of those examples for the class to be presented during the week we discuss the method. The best exemplars may be saved for use in subsequent classes.

Final project. Working in teams of three or four, and using any Problem Restatement and Divergent and Convergent Thinking plus at least three other methods developed in the course – for a total of of at least five methods – you will develop an operational project to be presented at the last class. You will apply the elements of critical thinking to the method chosen as well as the specific problem, apply the appropriate methods to solve of problem, report the results, and evaluate the process. The project will be presented during a 15–20 minute briefing. A list of the specific elements that must be included and the format by which the project is graded is on the last page of this syllabus.

Grading:

- **Written Summaries (25%).** Due weekly. The first summary will be graded. Subsequently, a random number generator will be used to select three (3) additional summaries for grading. Grading will be based on the "Universal Intellectual Standards" in *The Foundations of Analytic Thinking* and on whether instructions are followed. For example, if you are asked to identify what key questions an author is attempting to answer, *it is expected that you will provide those questions in the reading summary.*
- **Class Participation (25%).** Since this is a discussion course, you are expected to engage in the process.
- **Operational Exemplars (25%).** Assigned the first week. No longer than 5 minutes each.
- **Final Project (25%).**

Class Descriptions and Weekly Assignments (complete prior to each class):

Class 1 – How We Don't Think and How We Might

Reading Assignment: *The Thinker's Toolkit: Fourteen Skills for Making Smarter Decisions in Business and in Life,* Chapters 1–2 (Part One).
Psychology of Intelligence Analysis, 1–30.
Critical Thinking: Concepts and Tools, entire work.

Written Assignment: *Reading summaries for chapters from Jones and Heuer. Exercises in text.*

Class Objectives: *At the end of Class 1 you will be able to:*
- Define a bias and discuss the implications of biases in our decisions.
- Identify sources of cognitive biases.
- Describe the inherent dangers/benefits of biases and the difficulty of compensating for perceptual biases.
- Describe the characteristics and three principles of perception.
- Describe how analysts fall prey to absence-of-evidence biases.
- Describe how anchoring impacts analytical decision-making.
- Describe how a target can use assimilation biases to deceive.
- Acknowledge how analysts unwittingly use confirmation bias to support early assessments.
- Discuss how hindsight and reliability biases play a part in intelligence failures.
- Describe how oversensitivity to consistency bias can lead to undesirable results.
- Discuss how expert biases and the Pollyanna and Cassandra complexes distort our thinking.
- Describe how cultural, personal, and organizational

mindsets impact analysis.

- Define mindsets, discuss how they are derived, and describe how they influence predictions.
- Identify how we think.
- Describe critical thinking and the standards used for evaluating our thinking.
- Identify the elemental structures of thought.
- Describe the differences between inferences and assumptions in intelligence analysis.

Class 2 – Critical Problem Restatement and Alternative Thinking

Reading Assignment: *The Thinker's Toolkit: Fourteen Skills for Making Smarter Decisions in Business and in Life,* Chapters 3, 5.

Written Assignment: *Reading summaries for each chapter. Exercises in text.*

Class Objectives: *At the end of Class 2 you will be able to:*
- Demonstrate knowledge of the critical thinking process by providing an example that meets the universal intellectual standards.
- Describe the role of questioning in critical thinking.
- Identify the three types of questions used in critical thinking.
- Determine the sample domains involved in complex questions.
- Define problem restatement and apply its use through a practical example.
- Discuss the role that our biases play in problem restatement.
- Demonstrate knowledge of the critical thinking process by providing an example that meets the universal intellectual standards.
- Define divergent thinking and its benefits when performing a problem restatement.
- Discuss the pitfall involved in problem definition and how it relates to problem restatement.
- Describe some effective techniques for problem restatement.
- Identify the types of problems that benefit from problem restatement.
- Discuss how points of view influence the critical thinking process.
- Discuss the logic, benefits, risks, and elements of divergent thinking.
- Identify the four main ideas of divergent thinking.

- Describe what is needed to move from divergence to convergence.
- Identify the types of problems that benefit from divergent thinking.

Class 3 – Pollyanna, Cassandra, and Marshaling

Reading Assignment: *The Thinker's Toolkit: Fourteen Skills for Making Smarter Decisions in Business and in Life*, Chapters 4, 6.

Written Assignment: *Reading summaries for each chapter. Exercises in text.*

Class Objectives: *At the end of Class 3 you will be able to:*
- Discuss the pros-cons-fixes approach to critical thinking and the six-step method employed by successful analysts.
- Identify the logic behind the pros-cons-fixes approach and discuss those critical thinking problems best suited to this method.
- Apply the techniques of sorting, chronologies, and timelines to critical thinking and identify those critical thinking problems best suited for this approach.
- Identify the two-step technique used for sorted lists, chronologies, and timelines.

Class 4 – Causes, Squares, and Shrubs

Reading Assignment: *The Thinker's Toolkit: Fourteen Skills for Making Smarter Decisions in Business and in Life*, Chapters 7, 8, 9.

Written Assignment: *Reading summaries for each chapter. Exercises in text.*

Class Objectives: *At the end of Class 4 you will be able to:*
- Discuss the purpose, logic, underlying question, evidence, concepts, and types of problems best suited for causal flow diagramming.
- Identify the major factors and cause-and-effect relationships influencing causal flow diagramming.
- Characterize the differences between direct and inverse relationships and their impact on causal flow diagramming.
- Define a feedback loop and discuss what makes it stable or unstable.
- Apply your knowledge of causal diagramming by participating in a classroom exercise.
- Discuss the purpose, logic, underlying question, evidence, concepts, and types of problems best suited for scenario matrices and trees.
- Define and discuss the characteristics and differences between matrices and scenario trees.
- Apply your knowledge of scenario matrices by participating in a classroom exercise.
- Apply your knowledge of scenario trees by participating in a classroom exercise.

Class 5 – Weighing the Likelihood

Reading Assignment: *The Thinker's Toolkit: Fourteen Skills for Making Smarter Decisions in Business and in Life,* Chapters 10, 13.

Written Assignment: *Reading summaries for each chapter. Exercises in text.*

Class Objectives: *At the end of Class 5 you will be able to:*
- Discuss how individuals view issues.
- Discuss the purpose, logic, underlying question, evidence, concepts, and types of problems best suited for weighted ranking.
- List the 9-step process involved in weighted ranking.
- Demonstrate knowledge of weighted ranking through class and small group exercises.
- Discuss the purpose, logic, underlying question, evidence, concepts, and types of problems best suited for probability.
- Define and describe how and why we characterize and assign events, and how this influences intelligence analysis.
- Discuss and explain the differences between mutually exclusive and conditionally dependent events relative to probability.
- Identify the seven steps in creating a probability tree.
- Apply your knowledge of probability by participating in a classroom exercise.

Class 6 – Testing the Devil's and Other's Advocacy

Reading Assignment: *The Thinker's Toolkit: Fourteen Skills for Making Smarter Decisions in Business and in Life,* Chapters 11–12.
The Psychology of Intelligence Analysis, Chapter 8.

Written Assignment: *Reading summaries for each chapter. Exercises in text.*

Class Objectives: *At the end of Class 6 you will be able to:*
- Define intelligence.
- Discuss the purpose, logic, underlying question, evidence, concepts, and types of problems best suited for devil's advocacy.
- Define, describe, and characterize situations appropriate to employ methods of devil's advocacy in intelligence analysis
- Demonstrate prowess in devil's advocacy through participation in a practical case study.
- Discuss the purpose, logic, underlying question, evidence, concepts, and types of problems best suited for hypothesis testing.
- Discuss the benefits of hypothesis testing.
- Identify the 8-step process of hypothesis testing.
- Demonstrate prowess in hypothesis testing through participation in a practical case study.

Class 7 – Analyzing Apples and Toyotas

Reading Assignment: *The Thinker's Toolkit: Fourteen Skills for Making Smarter Decisions in Business and in Life*, Chapters 14, 15, 16.

Written Assignment: *Reading summaries for each chapter. Exercises in text.*

Class Objectives: *At the end of Class 7 you will be able to:*
- Describe how individual viewpoints influence utility analysis.
- Define utility analysis and discuss the type of problems best suited for this method.
- Identify the logic of utility analysis.
- Employ utility analysis to arrive at the most cost-effective solutions.
- List the steps involved in creating a utility tree and apply this knowledge by participating in classroom exercises.
- List the steps involved in creating a utility matrix and apply this knowledge by participating in classroom exercises.
- Examine the benefits of structuring as it applies to utility and probability analysis.
- Describe the differences between utility and probability analysis.
- Examine multi-perspective utility analysis and its use by participating in classroom exercises.
- List the 13 steps of multi-perspective utility analysis.
- Apply your knowledge of multi-perspective utility analysis by participating in a classroom exercise.

Class 8 – And Now for Something Completely Different

Reading Assignment: *Review all assigned readings.*

Written Assignment: *None.*

Class Objectives: *At the end of Class 8 you will be able to:*
- Describe which structured analysis methods work best in particular situations.
- Demonstrate knowledge of critical thinking and structured analysis through a practicum.
- Demonstrate your knowledge of critical thinking and structured analysis through a small group exercise.

Class 9 – Final Project Preparation

Reading Assignment: *Review all assigned readings.*

Written Assignment: *None.*

Class Objectives: *During Class 9 you will:*
- Learn through experience the pros and cons of research, analysis and reporting in small teams.

Class 10 – Final Project Presentation and Wrap-up

Reading Assignment: *Review all assigned readings.*

Written Assignment: *None.*

Class Objectives: *During Class 10:*
- Your small group will make a multi-media presentation on the analytic problem you chose.

Methods:
- A sample of the problem statement and restatement process.
- A sample of the convergent and divergent thinking applied to the problem.
- Concise demonstrations of the three structured analytic methods used to answer the analytic problem.

Assessment:
- **You are evaluated on how clearly the group presents its project, and on whether the project requirements listed above are met as shown on the last page of the syllabus.**

Reading Summary Questions:[231]

For each chapter/work, answer the following questions (in writing) about the reading.

1. What is the author's purpose? If there is more than one main point, what is the overarching purpose?

2. What are the key questions the author raises/addresses?

3. What evidence does the author provide to support his argument?

4. What inferences does the author make from the evidence?

5. On what underlying concepts does the author rely?

6. What does the author take for granted? What assumptions does the author make?

7. What are the implications of the author's point of view? What are the implications if we adopt/do not adopt what the author recommends?

8. What is the author's point of view? What other points of view are there?

---

231 Paul and Elder, *Concepts and Tools*, 13.

Final Project Evaluation Worksheet[232]

	Clarity	Accuracy	Precision	Relevance	Depth	Breadth	Logic	Significance	Fairness
Purpose									
Key Questions									
Assumptions									
Evidence									
A: Methods									
B: Analysis									
Concepts									
Inferences									
Implications									
Other Points of View									
Lessons Learned									
Comments									

232 Derived by author from Paul and Elder, *Concepts and Tools*, 2–9.

BIBLIOGRAPHY

Ackerman, Robert K. "Information Age Poses New Challenges to Intelligence." *Signal* 53, no. 2 (October 1998): 23–25.

Advanced Research and Development Activity. *Broad Agency Announcement for the Novel Intelligence from Massive Data (NIMD) R&D Program.* NMA-401-02-BAA-0004, 7 June 2002, 1.

_____. "Preliminary Solicitation Information for Advanced QUestion & Answering for INTelligence (AQUAINT)." URL: <http://www.digitalgovernment.org/library/library/pdf/preliminary_information.pdf>. Last accessed 26 March 2006.

Air Force Research Laboratory (AFRL). IFED Directorate. "Collaboration and Analyst/System Effectiveness (CASE)." BAA 06-02-IFKA, 28 October 2005. URL: <http://www.rl.af.mil/div/IFK/baa/>. Last accessed 11 March 2006.

Allen, Charles E. "Intelligence: Cult, Craft, or Business?" In *Seminar on Intelligence, Command, and Control, Guest Presentations, Spring 2000.* Cambridge, MA: Harvard University Program on Information Resources Policy, I-01-1, April 2000. URL: <http://www.pirp.harvard.edu/pubs.html>. Last accessed 11 January 2006.

Allison, Graham, and Philip Zelikow. *Essence of Decision: Explaining the Cuban Missile Crisis,* 2nd Edition. New York, NY: Longman, 1999.

Amuchastegui, Domingo "Cuban Intelligence and the October Crisis." In James G. Blight and David A. Welch, Eds. *Intelligence and the Cuban Missile Crisis.* London, UK: Frank Cass, 1998: 88–119.

Anderson, Terence J., and William Twining. *Analysis of Evidence: How to Do Things with Facts Based on Wigmore's Science of Judicial Proof.* Chicago, IL: Northwestern University Press, 1991.

Anderson, Terence J., David A. Schum, and William Twining. *Analysis of Evidence.* Cambridge, UK: Cambridge University Press, 2005.

Bathurst, Robert B. *Intelligence and the Mirror: On Creating an Enemy.* Oslo, Norway: International Peace Research Institute, 1993.

Ben-Israel, Isaac. "Philosophy and Methodology of Intelligence: The Logic of the Estimate Process. *Intelligence and National Security* 4, no. 4 (October 1989): 660–718.

Blight, James G., and David A. Welch, Eds. *Intelligence and the Cuban Missile Crisis.* London, UK: Frank Cass, 1998.

Boden, Margaret A. *The Creative Mind: Myths and Mechanisms.* New York, NY: Basic Books, 1990.

Brei, William S., CAPT, USAF. *Getting Intelligence Right: The Power of Logical Procedure.* Occasional Paper Number Two. Washington, DC: Joint Military Intelligence College, January 1996.

Brent, Joseph. *Charles Sanders Peirce: A Life.* Bloomington, IN: Indiana University Press, 1998.

Brookfield, Stephen D. *Developing Critical Thinkers: Challenging Adults to Explore Alternative Ways of Thinking and Acting.* San Francisco, CA: Jossey-Bass Publishers, 1987.

Callum, Robert. "The Case for Cultural Diversity in the Intelligence Community." *International Journal of Intelligence and CounterIntelligence* 14, no. 1, Spring 2001: 25–48.

Cheikes, Brant A., Mark J. Brown, Paul E. Lehner, and Leonard Adelman. *Confirmation Bias in Complex Analyses,* Mitre Technical Report MTR 04B0000017. Bedford, MA: Center for Integrated Intelligence Systems, October 2004.

Christensen, Clayton M. *The Innovator's Dilemma: When New Technologies Cause Great Firms to Fail.* Boston, MA: Harvard Business School Press, 1997.

Christensen, Clayton M., and Michael E. Raynor. *The Innovator's Solution: Creating and Sustaining Successful Growth.* Boston, MA: Harvard Business School Press, 2003.

Christensen, Clayton M., Scott D. Anthony, and Erik A. Roth. *Seeing What's Next: Using the Theories of Innovation to Predict Industry Change.* Boston, MA: Harvard Business School Press, 2004.

"Clarke: Bush Didn't See Terrorism as 'Urgent'." *CNN.com, 19* May 2004. URL: <http://www.cnn.com/2004/ALLPOLITICS/03/24/911.commission/index.htm>. Last accessed 9 March 2006.

Commission on the Intelligence Capabilities of the United States Regarding Weapons of Mass Destruction. *Report to the President of the United States.* Washington DC: Government Printing Office, March 31, 2005. URL: <http://www.wmd.gov/report/ index.html>, last accessed 28 July 2005.

Cooper, Jeffrey R. *Curing Analytic Pathologies: Pathways to Improved Intelligence Analysis.* Washington, DC: Center for the Study of Intelligence, 2005.

_____. Email to the author. 31 March 2006.

Davis, Jack. "The Kent-Kendall Debate of 1949." *Studies in Intelligence* 35, no. 2 (Summer 1991): 37–50.

De Bono, Edward. *de Bono's Thinking Course.* New York, NY: Facts on File Publications, 1982.

De Cagna, Jeff. "Making Change Happen: Steve Denning Tells the Story of Storytelling." *Information Outlook*, January 2001: 28–35.

De Rivera, Joseph. *The Psychological Dimension of Foreign Policy.* Columbus, OH: Charles E. Merrill Publishing Company, 1968.

Denning, Stephen. *The Springboard: How Storytelling Ignites Action in Knowledge-Era Organizations.* Boston, MA: Butterworth-Heinemann, 2001.

Devlin, Keith. *Goodbye Descartes: The End of Logic and the Search for a New Cosmology of the Mind.* New York, NY: John Wiley & Sons, Inc., 1997.

Dewey, John. *How We Think: A Restatement of the Relation of Reflective Thinking to the Educative Process.* New York, NY: D.C. Heath and Company, 1910.

Dijksterhuis, Ap, Martin W. Bos, Loran F. Nordgren, and Rick B. von Baren. "On Making the Right Choice: The Deliberation-Without-Attention Effect." *Science*, 311, no. 5763 (17 February 2006): 1005–1007.

DiSpezio, Michael A. *Classic Critical Thinking Puzzles.* New York, NY: Main Street, 2005.

Durkheim, Emile. *The Rules of Sociological Method.* Glencoe, IL: Free Press, 1938.

Eco, Umberto, and Thomas A. Sebeok. *The Sign of Three: Dupin, Holmes, Pierce.* Bloomington, IN: Indiana University Press, 1988

EDS. *Herding Cats.* Television advertisement produced for EDS by Fallon-McElligott. Videocassette, January 2000.

_____. *Building Airplanes in Flight*. Television advertisement produced for EDS by Fallon-McElligott. Videocassette, November 2000.

Elder, Linda, and Richard Paul. *The Foundations of Analytic Thinking: How to Take Thinking Apart and What to Look for When You Do.* Dillon Beach, CA: The Foundation for Critical Thinking, 2003.

Elliott, Michael. "How the U.S. Missed the Clues." *CNN.com*, 20 May 2002. URL: < http://archives.cnn.com/2002/ALLPOLITICS/05/20/time.clues/index.html>. Last accessed 9 March 2006.

Facione, Peter A. *Critical Thinking: What It Is and Why It Counts.* Milbrae, CA: California Academic Press, 1998, updated 2004. URL<http://www.insightassessment.com/>. Last accessed 22 July 2005.

Facione, Peter A., Noreen C. Facione, and Carol A. Giancarlo. "The Disposition Towards Critical Thinking: Its Character, Measurement, and Relationship to Critical Thinking Skill," *Informal Logic* 20, no. 1 (2000): 61–84.

_____. *Professional Judgment and the Disposition Toward Critical Thinking* (Milbrae, CA: California Academic Press, 2002). URL: < http://www.calpress.com/ pdf_files/Prof_jmn.pdf>. Last accessed 31 March 2006.

Feder, Stanley. "Factions and Policon: New Ways to Analyze Politics." In Westerfield, H. Bradford, ed. *Inside CIA's Private World: Declassified Articles from the Agency's Internal Journal, 1955–1992.* New Haven, CT: Yale University Press, 1995.

Feldman, Daniel. *Critical Thinking: Strategies for Decision Making.* Menlo Park, CA: Crisp Publications, Inc, 2002.

Fisher, Alec. *Critical Thinking: An Introduction.* Cambridge, UK: Cambridge University Press, 2001.

Folker, Robert D., MSGT, USAF. *Intelligence Analysis in Theater Joint Intelligence Centers: An Experiment in Applying Structured Methods.* Occasional Paper Number Seven. Washington, DC: Joint Military Intelligence College, January 2000.

Folker, Robert D., LT, USAF. Email to the author. 9 December 2003.

Fursenko, Aleksandr and Timothy Naftali. *"One Hell of a Gamble:" Khrushchev, Castro, and Kennedy, 1958–1964.* New York, NY: W. W. Norton & Company, 1997.

Garthoff, Raymond L. "US Intelligence in the Cuban Missile Crisis." In James G. Blight and David A. Welch, Eds. *Intelligence and the Cuban Missile Crisis.* London, UK: Frank Cass, 1998: 18–63.

George, Alexander. *Presidential Decisionmaking in Foreign Policy: The Effective Use of Information and Advice.* Boulder, CO: Westview Press, 1980.

Gilovich, Thomas. *How We Know What Isn't So: The Fallibility of Human Reason in Everyday Life.* New York, NY: The Free Press, 1991.

Gilovich, Thomas, Dale Griffin, and Daniel Kahneman, Eds. *Heuristics and Biases: The Psychology of Intuitive Judgment.* Cambridge, UK: Cambridge University Press, 2002.

Gladwell, Malcolm. *The Tipping Point: How Little Things Can Make a Big Difference.* Boston, MA: Little Brown and Company, 2000.

_____. *Blink: The Power of Thinking without Thinking.* Boston, MA: Little Brown and Company, 2005.

Glaser, Edward M. *An Experiment in the Development of Critical Thinking.* New York, NY: AMS Press, 1941.

Grabo, Cynthia M. *Anticipating Surprise: Analysis for Strategic Warning.* Washington DC: Joint Military Intelligence College, 2002.

Gribkov, Anatoli. "The View from Moscow and Havana." In Gribkov, Anatoli, and William Y. Smith. *Operation ANADYR: U.S. and Soviet Generals Recount the Cuban Missile Crisis.* Chicago, IL: Edition q, 1994: 3–76.

Gribkov, Anatoli, and William Y. Smith. *Operation ANADYR: U.S. and Soviet Generals Recount the Cuban Missile Crisis.* Chicago, IL: Edition q, 1994.

Halpern, Diane. *Thought and Knowledge: An Introduction to Critical Thinking,* 4th Edition. Mahwah, NJ: Lawrence Erlbaum Associates, Publishers, 2002.

Hampson, Fen Osler. "The Divided Decision-Maker: American Domestic Politics and the Cuban Crises." *International Security,* 9, no 3 (Winter 1984/85): 130-165.

Harcourt Assessment, Inc. *Local Norms Report, Watson-Glaser Critical Thinking Assessment.* Report prepared for the Defense Intelligence Agency, 2005.

Heuer, Richards J., Jr. "Strategic Deception and Counterdeception: A Cognitive Process Approach." *International Studies Quarterly* 25, no. 2 (June 1981): 294–327.

_____. *Adapting Academic Methods and Models to Governmental Needs: The CIA Experience.* Strategic Studies Institute. U.S. Army War College. July 31, 1978.

_____. *Psychology of Intelligence Analysis.* Washington, DC: CIA Center for the Study of Intelligence, 1999.

Hinsley, F. H., and Alan Stripp, Eds. *Codebreakers: The Inside Story of Bletchley Park.* Oxford, UK: Oxford University Press, 1993.

Holyoak, Keith J., and Paul Thagard. *Mental Leaps: Analogy in Creative Thought.* Cambridge, MA: The MIT Press, 1995.

Hughes, Francis J. Conversation with the author. Washington, DC: Joint Military Intelligence College. 8 May 2003.

Hughes, Francis J., and David A. Schum. *Credibility Assessment: A First Step in Intelligence Analysis*. Unpublished tutorial. Joint Military Intelligence College, April 2003.

Janis, Irving. *Groupthink: Psychological Studies of Policy Decisions and Fiascoes*, 2nd Edition. Boston, MA: Houghton Mifflin Company, 1982.

Jervis, Robert. *System Effects: Complexity in Political and Social Life*. Princeton, NJ: Princeton University Press, 1997.

Johnson Thomas R., and David A. Hatch. *NSA and the Cuban Missile Crisis*. Fort Meade, MD: National Security Agency Center for Cryptologic History, 1998. URL: <http://www.nsa.gov/publications/publi00033.cfm>. Accessed 18 April 2006

Johnston, Rob. *Analytic Culture in the U.S. Intelligence Community: An Ethnographic Study*. Washington, DC: Center for the Study of Intelligence, 2005.

Jones, Morgan D. *The Thinker's Toolkit: 14 Powerful Techniques for Problem Solving*. New York, NY: Random House, Inc, 1995.

_____. Conversation with the author. 15 December 2003.

Kahneman, Daniel, Paul Slovic, and Amos Tversky, eds. *Judgment under Uncertainty: Heuristics and Biases*. Cambridge, UK: Cambridge University Press, 1982.

Kam, Ephraim. *Surprise Attack: The Victim's Perspective*. Cambridge, MA: Harvard University Press, 1990.

Kent, Sherman. *Strategic Intelligence for American World Policy*. Princeton, NJ: Princeton University Press, 1949.

_____. "A Crucial Estimate Relived." *Studies in Intelligence* 36, no. 5 (1992): 111–119.

Kerbel, Josh. "Thinking Straight: Cognitive Bias in the US Debate about China." *Studies in Intelligence* 48, no. 3 (2004), URL: <http://cia.gov/csi/studies/vol48no3/index.html>. Last accessed 22 February 2006.

Klein, Gary. *Intuition at Work: Why Developing Your Gut Instincts Will Make You Better at What You Do.* New York, NY: Doubleday, 2003.

Krizan, Lisa. *Intelligence Essentials for Everyone.* Occasional Paper Number Six. Washington, DC: Joint Military Intelligence College, 1999.

Lebow, Richard Ned, and Janice Gross Stein. "Back to the Past: Counterfactuals and the Cuban Missile Crisis." In Philip E. Tetlock, and Aaron Belkin *Counterfactual Thought Experiments in World Politics: Logical, Methodological, and Psychological Perspectives.* Princeton, NJ: Princeton University Press, 1996: 119–148.

LeGault, Michael R. *Think: Why Crucial Decisions Can't Be Made in the Blink of an Eye.* New York, NY: Threshold Editions, 2006.

Lengel, Allan. "Little Progress in FBI Probe of Anthrax Attacks: Internal Report Compiled As Agents Hope for a Break." *Washington Post.* 16 September 2005. A01.

Lengel, Allan, and Guy Gugliotta. "Md. Pond Produces No Anthrax Microbes: FBI Sought Clues In Deadly Attacks." *Washington Post.* 1 August 2003. A03.

Lipman, Matthew. *Thinking in Education*, 2nd Edition. Cambridge, UK: Cambridge University Press, 2003.

Lundahl, Arthur C. "Additional Information—Mission 3102." Memorandum for Director of Central Intelligence and Director, Defense Intelligence Agency, 15 October 1962. In Mary S. McAuliffe, ed., *CIA Documents on the Cuban Missile Crisis, 1962.* Washington DC: Central Intelligence Agency, 1992: 181–182.

_____. "Additional Information—Mission 3107." Memorandum for Director of Central Intelligence and Director, Defense Intelligence Agency, 19 October 1962. In Mary S. McAuliffe, ed., *CIA Documents on the Cuban Missile Crisis, 1962.* Washington DC: Central Intelligence Agency, 1992: 209.

McAuliffe, Mary S., ed. *CIA Documents on the Cuban Missile Crisis, 1962* Washington DC: Central Intelligence Agency, 1992.

Marrin, Stephen. "Homeland Security and the Analysis of Foreign Intelligence," Markle Foundation Task Force on National Security in the Information Age, 15 July 2002, URL: <www.markletaskforce.org/documents/marrin_071502.pdf>. Last accessed December 9, 2003.

_____. Email to the author, 8 December 2003.

_____. "CIA's Kent School: Improving Training for New Analysts." *International Journal of Intelligence and CounterIntelligence* 16, no. 4 (Winter 2003–2004): 609–637.

May, Ernest R. *Lessons of the Past: The Use and Misuse of History in American Foreign Policy.* Oxford, UK: Oxford University Press, 1973.

Merom, Gil. "The 1962 Cuban Intelligence Estimate: A Methodological Perspective." *Intelligence and National Security,* 14, no. 3 (Autumn 1999): 48–80.

Mid-Level Intelligence Professional. National Security Agency. Email to the author, 9 March 2006.

Miller, George A. "The Magical Number Seven, Plus or Minus Two." *The Psychological Review* 63 (1956): 81–97.

Miller, Judith. "A Battle of Words over War Intelligence." *New York Times*. Online edition, 22 November 2003. URL: <www.nytimes.com/2003/11/22/arts/22INTE.html>. Last accessed November 28, 2003.

Millward, William. "Life in and out of Hut 3." In Hinsley, F. H., and Alan Stripp, Eds. *Codebreakers: The Inside Story of Bletchley Park*. Oxford, UK: Oxford University Press, 1993: 17–29.

Moore, David T. *Creating Intelligence: Evidence and Inference in the Analysis Process*. MSSI Thesis. Washington, DC: Joint Military Intelligence College, July 2002.

_____. "Species of Competencies for Intelligence Analysis." *Defense Intelligence Journal* 11, no. 2 (Summer 2002): 97–119.

_____. Personal Notes. Joint Military Intelligence College, Denial and Deception Advanced Studies Program, Spring 2005.

Moore David T., and Lisa Krizan. "Intelligence Analysis: Does NSA Have What it Takes." Reprint: NSA Center for Cryptologic History. *Cryptologic Quarterly*, 20, nos 1/2 (Summer/Fall 2001): 1–33.

_____. "Core Competencies for Intelligence Analysis at the National Security Agency." In Swenson, Russell G., ed. *Bringing Intelligence About: Practitioners Reflect on Best Practices*. Washington DC: Joint Intelligence Military College, 2003: 95–132.

Moore, David T., Lisa Krizan, and Elizabeth J. Moore. "Evaluating Intelligence: A Competency-Based Model." *International Journal of Intelligence and Counterintelligence* 18, no. 2 (Summer 2005): 204–220.

Myers, David G. *Intuition: Its Powers and Perils*. New Haven, CT: Yale University Press, 2002.

Negroponte, John D., Director of National Intelligence. *National Intelligence Strategy of the United States of America.* Washington, DC: Office of the Director of National Intelligence, October 2005. URL: <http://www.dni.gov/NISOctober2005.pdf>. Last accessed 12 March 2006.

Neustadt, Richard E., and Ernest R. May. *Thinking in Time: The Uses of History for Decision Makers.* New York, NY: The Free Press, 1986.

Oberdorfer, Don. "Missed Signals in the Middle East." *Washington Post Magazine*, 17 March 1991.

Paul, Richard W. "A Draft Statement of Principles." The National Council for Excellence in Critical Thinking. URL: <www.criticalthinking.org/ncect.html>. Last accessed March 18, 2003.

Paul, Richard W., and Linda Elder. *The Miniature Guide to Critical Thinking Concepts and Tools*, 4th Edition. Dillon Beach, CA: The Foundation for Critical Thinking, 2004.

Paul, Richard W., and Gerald Nosich. *A Model for the National Assessment of Higher Order Thinking.* Dillon Beach, CA: Foundation for Critical Thinking, n.d.

Paul, Richard W., Linda Elder, and Ted Bartell. "Executive Summary, Study of 38 Public Universities and 28 Private Universities To Determine Faculty Emphasis on Critical Thinking In Instruction." *California Teacher Preparation for Instruction in Critical Thinking: Research Findings and Policy Recommendations.* California Commission on Teacher Credentialing, Sacramento, California, 1997. Dillon, CA: Foundation for Critical Thinking, 1997. URL: <criticalthinking.org/schoolstudy.htm>. Last accessed March 18, 2003.

Paul, Richard W., Linda Elder, and Ted Bartell. *California Teacher Preparation for Instruction in Critical Thinking: Research Findings and Policy Recommendations.* California Commission on Teacher Credentialing, Sacramento California, 1997. Dillon, CA: Foundation for Critical Thinking, 1997.

Perrow, Charles. *Normal Accidents: Living with High-Risk Technologies.* Princeton, NJ: Princeton University Press, 1999.

Pettee, George S. *The Future of American Secret Intelligence.* Washington, DC: Infantry Journal Press, 1946.

Platt, Washington. *Strategic Intelligence Production: Basic Principles.* New York, NY: Frederick A. Praeger, 1957.

Plous, Scott. *The Psychology of Judgment and Decision-Making.* New York, NY: McGraw Hill, Inc., 1993.

Raasa, Paul J. "The Denial and Deception Challenge to Intelligence." In Godson, Roy, and James J. Wirtz, *Strategic Denial and Deception.* New Brunswick, NJ: Transaction Publishers, 2002: 223–228.

Reed, Jennifer H. *Effect of a Model For Critical Thinking on Student Achievement In Primary Source Document Analysis And Interpretation, Argumentative Reasoning, Critical Thinking Dispositions, and History Content in a Community College History Course.* PhD Dissertation. College of Education, University of South Florida, December 1998. URL: <http://www.criticalthinking.org/resources/JReed-Dissertation.pdf>. Last accessed 6 May 2006.

Restak, Richard, M.D. *The Brain Has a Mind of Its Own: Insights from a Practicing Neurologist.* New York, NY: Harmony Books, 1991.

Reynolds, William. Conversation with the author, 14 March 2006.

Rieber, Steven, and Neil Thomason. "Toward Improving Intelligence Analysis: Creation of a National Institute for Analytic Methods." *Studies in Intelligence* 49, no. 4 (Winter 2006): 71–80.

Schafersman, Steven D. "An Introduction to Critical Thinking," January 1991. URL: <www.freeinquiry.com/critical-thinking. html>. Last accessed 9 March 2006.

Schecter Jerrold L., and Peter S. Deriabin. *The Spy Who Saved the World.* New York, NY: Scribner's, 1992.

Schum, David A. *Evidence and Inference for the Intelligence Analyst,* 2 volumes. Lanham, MD: University Press of America, 1987.

_____. *Evidential Foundations of Probabilistic Reasoning.* New York, NY: John Wiley & Sons, Inc., 1994.

_____. "Species of Abductive Reasoning in Fact Investigation in Law" *Cardozo Law Review* 22, nos. 5/6 (July 2001): 1645–1681.

_____. "Evidence Marshaling for Imaginative Fact Investigation." *Artificial Intelligence and Law* 9 (2001): 165–188.

Sebeok, Thomas A. "One, Two, Three Spells UBERTY." In Umberto Eco and Thomas A. Sebeok. *The Sign of Three: Dupin, Holmes, Pierce.* Bloomington, IN: Indiana University Press, 1988: 1–10.

Senate Select Committee On Intelligence. *Report on the U.S. Intelligence Community's Prewar Intelligence Assessments on Iraq.* United States Senate. 108th Congress, 7 July 2004.

Simon, Herbert A. "Invariants of Human Behavior." *Annual Review of Psychology* 41 (1990):1–19.

Stefik, Mark, and Barbara Stefik. *Breakthrough: Stories and Strategies of Radical Innovation.* Cambridge, MA: MIT Press, 2004.

Swenson, Russell G., ed. *Research: Design and Methods.* Washington, DC: Joint Intelligence Military College, 2000.

_____. *Bringing Intelligence About: Practitioners Reflect on Best Practices.* Washington, DC: Joint Intelligence Military College, 2003.

Tetlock, Philip E. *Expert Political Judgment: How Good Is It? How Can We Know?* Princeton, NJ: Princeton University Press, 2005.

Tetlock, Philip E. and Aaron Belkin. *Counterfactual Thought Experiments in World Politics: Logical, Methodological, and Psychological Perspectives.* Princeton, NJ: Princeton University Press, 1996.

Thagard, Paul. *Coherence in Thought and Action.* Cambridge, MA: The MIT Press, 2000.

Treverton, Gregory F. Conversation with the author, 18 May 2006.

_____. Email exchanges with the author, 17–18 May 2006.

U.S. Congress. *Joint Inquiry into Intelligence Community Activities Before and After the Terrorist Attacks of September 11, 2001.* Report of the U.S. Senate Select Committee on Intelligence and U.S. House Permanent Select Committee on Intelligence, Together with Additional Views. Senate Report No. 107-351/House Report. No. 107-792. 107th Congress, 2nd Session. December 2002.

U.S. Department of Defense. Photograph in the John Fitzgerald Kennedy Library. Boston, MA. PX 66-20:7 14 October 1962.

White, Mark J. *Missiles in Cuba: Kennedy, Khrushchev, Castro, and the 1962 Crisis.* Chicago, IL: Ivan R. Dee, 1997.

Wikipedia. "The Free Encyclopedia." URL: <www.wkikpedia.org>. Last accessed 12 March 2006.

Wirtz, James J. "Organizing for Crisis Intelligence: Lessons form the Cuban Missile Crisis." In James G. Blight and David A. Welch, Eds. *Intelligence and the Cuban Missile Crisis.* London, UK: Frank Cass, 1998: 120–149.

Wohlstetter, Roberta. "Cuba and Pearl Harbor: Hindsight and Foresight." *Foreign Affairs* 46, no. 3 (July 1965): 691–707.

Woods, Kevin, James Lacey, and Williamson Murray. "Saddam's Delusions: The View from the Inside," *Foreign Affairs*, 85, no. 3 (May/June 2006). URL: <http://www.foreignaffairs. org/20060501faessay85301/kevin-woods-james-lacey-williamson-murray/saddam-s-delusions-the-view-from-the-inside.html>. Accessed 31 March 2006.

Woods, Kevin M., Michael R. Pease, Mark E. Stout, Williamson Murray, and James G. Lacey, *Iraqi Perspectives Project: A View of Operation Iraqi Freedom from Saddam's Senior Leadership.* Norfolk, VA: Joint Center for Operational Analysis, 2006. URL: <http://www.foreignaffairs.org/special/iraq/ipp.pdf>. Last accessed 31 March 2006.

Zlotnick, Jack. "Bayes' Theorem for Intelligence Analysis." *Studies in Intelligence* 11, no. 4 (Spring 1972): 1–12. URL: <http:// cia.gov/csi/kent_csi/pdf/v08i4a11p.pdf#page=1>. Last accessed 7 April 2006.

About the Author

DAVID T. MOORE is a career senior intelligence analyst and technical director at the National Security Agency where he is an advocate for, and mentor of best practices in intelligence analysis. He is an adjunct faculty member of the National Cryptologic School; has taught at the National Defense Intelligence College, Washington, DC; and at Trinity University, Washington, DC. Mr. Moore holds a B.A. in sociology from Washington and Lee University and a Master of Science of Strategic Intelligence from the National Defense Intelligence College (formerly the Joint Military Intelligence College).

Mr. Moore's other publications include:
- "Species of Competencies for Intelligence Analysis," *Defense Intelligence Journal*, 11, no. 2 (Summer 2002): 97-119.
- "Species of Competencies for Intelligence Analysis," *American Intelligence Journal*, 23 (2005): 29–43 (an expanded version of the original article).
- With coauthor Lisa Krizan:
  - "Intelligence Analysis, Does NSA Have What it Takes," *Cryptologic Quarterly*, 20, nos. 1/2 (Summer/Fall 2001): 1-32.
  - "Core Competencies for Intelligence Analysis at the National Security Agency," in *Bringing Intelligence About: Practitioners Reflect on Best Practices*, Russell Swenson, ed. (2004): 95-131.
- With coauthors Lisa Krizan and Elizabeth J. Moore
  - "Evaluating Intelligence: A Competency-Based Approach," in the *International Journal of Intelligence and CounterIntelligence*, 18, no. 2 (Summer 2005): 204-220.
- With coauthor William N. Reynolds:
  - "So Many Ways To Lie: The Complexity of Denial and Deception," *Defense Intelligence Journal*, 15, no. 2 (Fall 2006): 95-116.

CPSIA information can be obtained
at www.ICGtesting.com
Printed in the USA
BVHW040747220821
614864BV00003B/78